The Games Book

20 Board Games for General and Business English

by
Ann Schmid

Ernst Klett Verlag
Stuttgart Düsseldorf Leipzig

The Games Book
20 Board Games for General and Business English

by
Ann Schmid

Printed on
environmentally-friendly paper.

Ist edition   1 4 3 2 1 | 2001 2000 1999 1998

Acknowledgements:
The cartoons are reproduced by kind permission of
PUNCH (pp. 13, 26, 72, 89, 101) and THE SPECTATOR (p. 42)

Editor: David Shallis
Cover: Hanjo Schmidt

Printed by: Druckerei Wilhelm Röck, Weinsberg.
Printed in Germany.

ISBN 3-12-537931-8

Contents

Introduction

What sort of games?

The Games Book is designed for teachers working with adult learners of English. The twenty games in the collection are divided into two sections: ten for use with **general English** learners and ten more specifically for **business English** classes.

Teachers of business people will also want to use a number of the general English games: most classes will enjoy giving their views in *The Sports Game* (whether they are pro-sport or contra), and have fun polishing their shopping language in *The Department Store Game*. And they'll probably have plenty to say about celebrities and others in *The People Game*, too.

Games with adults?

However motivated and hard-working they are, adult learners also enjoy the chance to practise language in a more relaxed format, and the competitive element can be surprisingly productive. This is especially true for classes who have their lessons at the end of a hard day at work. "I'm glad my secretary can't see me," said a manager as he excitedly shouted out the answers during one of these games!

Levels and language

Each of the games in *The Games Book* has a **minimum starting level**, but beyond that they are open-ended, allowing more advanced learners to come up with whatever they can. The **language** overview section lets you see at a glance whether your class is ready for a particular game and a **key** suggests what minimum-level learners can be expected to come up with.

How to use the games

The games in *The Games Book* can be used in several ways:

1. as a **diagnostic test** at the start of a course, to see exactly what your learners' weaknesses are and how you can help, especially if you are teaching false beginners or a refresher course;

2. to **practise** a specific structure or topic that you have been teaching; blank cards at the back of the book allow you to personalize the material to fit your particular class;

3. to **revise** language you have taught at the beginning of the next lesson, or at any later stage of a course;

4. to **round off** a course before a break: *The Holiday Game*, for instance, makes an excellent way to wind up for the summer, and *The Christmas Game* settles one nicely into the festive spirit.

And there is no reason why many of the games should not also be **re-used** with the same learners at a later date, showing them just how much progress they've made since the last time!

How long do they take to play?

If you have taught something and want to use a game to practise it in the same lesson, allow at least **thirty minutes** for the game itself and a bit more time for feedback afterwards (see page 5).

Cutting a game short when learners are really getting into it can be frustrating. If it is clear that no one will reach the end of the board within a reasonable amount of time, set a **time limit**; the winner will then be the player who has made the most moves.

What about preparation?

Before using a game, check the language section and key to make sure it is appropriate for your class, then **try out a few moves** on the board to help you explain the rules. If you want to personalize the game to your class, use the blank cards at the back of the book.

Look at the "You will need" section and ensure that you have made all the necessary **copies** and cut up the **card sets**. Don't forget the **dice** (emergency substitute: six small squares of card, numbered from 1 to 6). Borrow the **markers** from family board games, or supply a selection of coins, keys, rings, etc. for learners to choose from.

Starting the game

1. **Explain why** learners are going to play the game: to help you establish their needs; to practise or revise a specific area of language; to allow them to test their general communicative competence.

2. Point out that **you will not correct** what learners say *during* the game; the aim here is extended fluency practice. If learners disagree as to the correctness of a response, or really need help with a particular point, they can of course ask you.

3. **Demonstrate the game** yourself by making a few moves on the board and asking learners to come up with suitable responses. You might want to check that they really understand how to play by asking one of them to explain the rules after you have done so.

During and after the game

Encourage learners to **judge their own performance** during the game rather than constantly turning to you for approval. If procedure is in doubt (for example, if a task seems ambiguous), let them decide what to do themselves.

Observe the play and **note anything interesting** that comes up, such as especially effective responses, or communication problems that the whole class need to be aware of so that they can avoid them in future.

Give feedback after the game: praise and then draw attention to a few useful points. Avoid a detailed examination of everything that went wrong – which could make learners wish they had never played the game in the first place!

And now, have fun!

The author

Acknowledgement
The author would like to mention that it was "Tell us about" in Friedericke Klippel's *Keep Talking* (CUP 1984) that started her interest in using board games in language classes and led to this collection.

General
English Games

The Adjectives Game

a General English game

In this game learners practice using adjectives, comparative and superlative forms.

Language

Level
from elementary

Vocabulary
Any vocabulary you want to test (see the cards on pages 10–11 for a selection of topics).

Preparation

Before the lesson
Decide whether you want to use the cards on pages 10–11 or make your own using the blank cards on page 112.

You will need
- one A3-size photocopy of the board on page 9 per group of 4–6 learners;
- one cut-up set of the cards on pages 10–11 (or your own cards) per group;
- one dice per group;
- one marker per player.

The Game

Introduction
Divide learners into groups of 4–6 players. Give each group a board, dice, markers and a set of cards.

Ask learners to gather round one board. Place the cards face down on the board. Demonstrate the game by making one or two moves and eliciting appropriate responses (see **Key** for suggestions).

The aim of the game
The winner is the first player to a) gain 50 points and then b) throw a 6 to get off the board (in any direction).

How to play
Players place their markers in the middle of the board. The first player to throw a 6 begins. Players take it in turns to throw the dice and move in any direction.

Players landing on a patterned circle take the top card from the pack, read it out and make a sentence related to the topic on the card.

Each sentence must include an adjective, or its comparative or superlative form, depending on the pattern of the circle they are on (see the legend on the edge of the board).

If the rest of the group approves of the sentence, the player gains the points for that pattern (again, see the board).

Players landing on a blank circle may not pick up a card.

Key
(some possible responses)

Card:	animals
Adjective:	*I've got a fat cat; My friend's got a black dog.*
Comparative:	*Elephants have larger ears than …*
Superlative:	*The largest animal in the world is …*
Card:	towns
Adjective:	*Our town isn't very large.*
Comparative:	*Paris is more beautiful than …*
Superlative:	*The most expensive city I know is …*
Card:	weather
Adjective:	*February was very cold this year.*
Comparative:	*The weather last summer was worse than the year before.*
Superlative:	*… is usually the hottest region here in summer.*

Alternative games
(from lower intermediate)

This game could be played in the same way using adverbs, nouns or verbs instead of adjectives:

1. Adverbs

Card:	work
Adverb:	*She works very hard/fast.*
Comparison:	*She types faster than/more slowly than …*
Superlative:	*She types the fastest …*

2. Nouns

Card:	appearance (points could be given for the number of related words in the sentence) *He's tall, quite thin and has brown curly hair.* (5 points)

3. Verbs

Card:	housework (points could be given for the number of related words in the sentence) *I did the ironing, dusted, washed the dishes and hoovered yesterday.* (4 points)

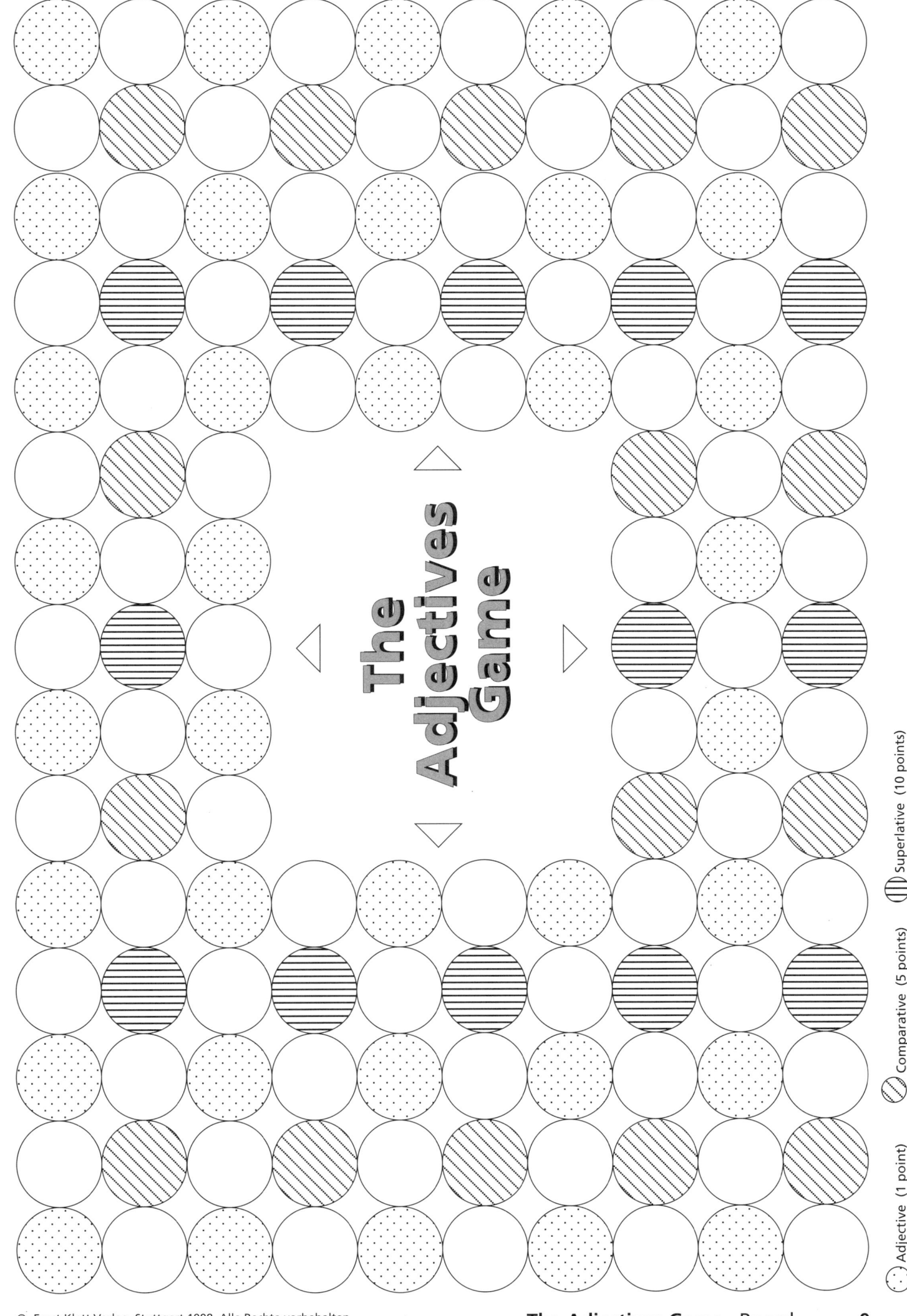

The Adjectives Game

Superlative (10 points)

Comparative (5 points)

Adjective (1 point)

The Adjectives Game · Board

animals	appearance	clothing
dislikes	drinks	education
enter-tainment	families	feelings
food	friends	furniture
health	hobbies	holidays
homes	hotels	housework

interests	likes	meals
music	nature	people
places	restaurants	shopping
sight-seeing	smoking	sport
technology	towns	transport
travel	weather	work

The Christmas Game

a General English game

In this game learners practise the language of social interaction at Christmas-time.

Language

Level
from intermediate

Some Christmas vocabulary
Decorations: *balls, candles, fairy lights, holly, mistletoe, streamers, tinsel, tree*
Food: *roast turkey, Christmas pudding, mince pies, Christmas cake*
Presents, etc: *Christmas card, Father Christmas/ Santa Claus, stocking, Christmas present, wrapping paper, Christmas cracker*
Season: *Advent, Christmas Eve, Christmas Day, Boxing Day*
Other: *Christmas carol*

Functions
- describing customs and habits
- describing dishes
- giving opinions, agreeing and disagreeing
- making, accepting and refusing invitations
- regretting
- speculating
- suggesting
- thanking

Preparation

Before the lesson
Decide whether you want to use the cards on page 15 or make your own using the blank cards on page 112.

You will need
- one A3-size photocopy of the board on page 14 per group of 4–6 learners;
- one cut-up set of the cards on page 15 (or your own cards) per group;
- one dice per group;
- one marker per player.

The Game

Introduction
Divide learners into groups of 4–6 players. Give each group a board, dice, markers and a set of cards.

Ask learners to gather round one board. Place the cards face down on the board. Demonstrate the game by making one or two moves and eliciting appropriate responses (see **Key** for suggestions).

The aim of the game
The winner is the first player to reach FINISH. You may wish to set a time limit rather than wait for a player to reach the final square; the winner is then the player who has made the most moves.

How to play
Players place their markers on START. The first player to throw a 6 begins. Players take it in turns to throw the dice and move around the board.

Players landing on a normal square read out the text and respond accordingly. If the rest of the group approve of the response, the game proceeds; if not, the player returns to his or her previous position.

Players landing on a square with a "Present" symbol take the top card from the pack, read it out and suggest an appropriate present, e.g.

Present card: An aunt who has three cats.
Suggestion: I'd buy her a lot of cat food.

Present card: A teenage boy.
Suggestion: *What about a computer game or a book?*

Key
(some possible responses)

1. Invite someone to have Christmas Dinner with you.
   Would you like to have Christmas Dinner with us?

2. You are the only person at a Christmas party wearing jeans.
   - *I'd go home and change – if I lived nearby!*
   - *I'd tell my hosts that I didn't realize that it was a formal party.*

3. Refuse an invitation to a Christmas drinks party.
   It's very kind of you, but I'm afraid I can't come. I have to …

4. What ingredients do you need to make a Christmas pudding?
   - *I've no idea – does anybody know?*
   - *I think you need sultanas, nuts, flour and spices.*

6 .Talk about spending Christmas in a hot country.
   It wouldn't be Christmas! For me, Christmas has to be winter, with the cold and snow.

7. English-speaking neighbours visit you unexpectedly on Christmas Eve.
    Hello! What a surprise! Please come in. Would you like a cup of coffee?

8. Describe a local Christmas dish.
    We always have … on Christmas Eve. It's made from …

10. Your family wants to stop giving Christmas presents. You don't.
    We do spend a lot of money on presents, but we must give presents to the children.

11. A relative you don't like very much has invited herself for Christmas.
    • *I wouldn't be very happy about it.*
    • *Oh, what a pity! I'm going away this Christmas.*

12. You think all Christmas trees should be made of plastic.
    So many trees are cut down every year just so that people can use them for a few days. There won't be any trees left soon!

14. You don't agree with using Christmas wrapping paper.
    What a waste of paper! You unwrap the present and throw away the paper. Think of all the trees …

15. A friend has given you a very expensive present.
    It's really lovely, but you shouldn't have spent so much money.

16. Accept an invitation to a Christmas party.
    That's very kind of you. I'd love to come.

17. Give an example of local Christmas biscuits or cakes.
    We have mince pies. They're made of pastry and filled with a sweet mixture of raisins, apples, nuts and spices.

19. Describe a local Christmas custom.
    We decorate all the pictures with holly – green leaves with red berries …

20. Thank your English hosts at the end of a Boxing Day meal at their house.
    Thank you very much. We really enjoyed the meal.

21. Your family wants to watch TV on Christmas Day. You don't.
    You watch TV every day. You don't have to watch it today. Everybody's here. We could do something different.

23. Someone you have invited to Christmas Dinner says she is vegetarian.
    Oh, dear! Shall I make you an omelette?

24. Describe a foreign Christmas custom.
    Well, in America they decorate the outside of the house and the garden with life-size Father Christmases.

26. You have received a present you don't like. Say thank you.
    Er, thank you so much. What a lovely …

27. Your family wants to spend Christmas at a hotel. You don't.
    Christmas should be spent at home – it's for families and children.

28. Your visitors want to go to church on Christmas Day. You don't.
    I'd come with you, but I have to cook the dinner. I'll drive you there and you could walk back.

29. You'd like to help others this Christmas.
    I think we should donate some money to a charity this year, instead of buying everybody presents they don't want.

30. Describe your most unusual Christmas.
    I once spent Christmas in Kenya …

"Well, we won't have needles all over the carpet."

THE CHRISTMAS GAME

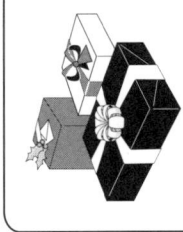

START

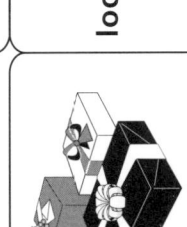

Invite someone to have Christmas Dinner with you.

You are the only person at a Christmas party wearing jeans.

Refuse an invitation to a Christmas drinks party.

What ingredients do you need to make a Christmas Pudding?

Someone you have invited to Christmas Dinner says she is a vegetarian.

Describe a foreign Christmas custom.

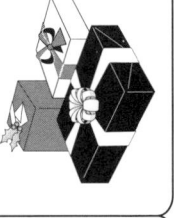

You have received a present you don't like. Say thank you.

Your family wants to spend Christmas at a hotel. You don't.

Your visitors want to go to church on Christmas Day. You don't.

Your family wants to watch TV on Christmas Day. You don't.

Thank your English hosts at the end of a Boxing Day meal at their house.

Describe a local Christmas custom.

Describe a local Christmas dish.

Your family wants to stop giving Christmas presents. You don't.

A relative you don't like very much has invited herself for Christmas.

You think all Christmas trees should be made of plastic.

Talk about spending Christmas in a hot country.

English-speaking neighbours visit you unexpectedly on Christmas Eve.

FINISH

Describe your most unusual Christmas.

You'd like to help others this Christmas.

GAME

Give an example of local Christmas biscuits or cakes.

Accept an invitation to a Christmas party.

A friend has given you a very expensive present.

You don't agree with using Christmas wrapping paper.

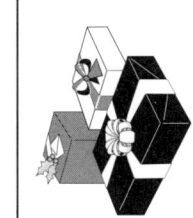

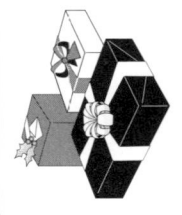

An aunt who has three cats.

A teenage boy.

A neighbour who looks after your house when you are on holiday.

A baby-sitter.

A French friend.

A friend who is a football fan.

A niece who loves pop music.

Parents-in-law who travel a lot.

A sister who works in a bookshop.

A ten-year-old brother.

A cousin in America.

A godson of 6 months.

A four-year-old nephew.

A rich friend.

A newly-married couple.

A helpful colleague at work.

An 86-year-old uncle who lives alone in a cottage in the country.

Your English teacher.

The Department Store Game

a General English game

In this game learners practise language for shopping.

Language

Level
from lower intermediate

Vocabulary
- names of store departments (see board)
- items typically sold in stores (see *Shopping lists*)

Functions
- asking about price and quality
- asking about size and colour
- asking for a service or object
- asking for directions
- asking for help and information

Preparation

Before the lesson
Decide whether you want to use the cards on page 19 or make your own using the blank cards on page 112.

You will need
- one A3-size photocopy of the board on page 17 per group of 4–6 learners;
- one cut-up set of the *Shopping lists* on page 18 and the *Excuse me* cards on page 19 per group;
- one dice per group;
- one marker per player.

The Game

Introduction
Divide learners into groups of 4–6 players. Give each group a board, dice, markers and a set of *Excuse me* cards.

Ask learners to gather round one board. Place the cards face down on the board. Demonstrate the game by making one or two moves and eliciting appropriate responses (see **Key** for some examples).

The aim of the game
The winner is the first player to tick off at least 6 things from his or her *Shopping list* before reaching the restaurant on the 5th floor. You may wish to set a time limit rather than wait for a player to reach the end of the board. The winner is then the player who has ticked off the most things.

How to play
Each player takes a *Shopping list* and chooses a partner for the game. Ask them to check their lists and the departments on the board for new vocabulary before starting the game.

Players place their markers on START. The first player to throw a 6 begins. Players take it in turns to throw the dice and move around the board.

When players land on a blank square, they have to buy something on their *Shopping list* in a department on that floor (see board). They do this by interacting with their partner, who plays the shop assistant.

Players landing on an *Excuse me* square take the top card from the pack, read it out and carry out the task, interacting with their partner as required. In some cases learners will have to decide themselves where something could be in the store.

Key
(some examples)

Blank squares

A player has *Shopping list 3* and lands on a blank square on the second floor.

Player: *Excuse me. Is this the latest Barbie?*
Partner: *Yes, that's right. This is the latest one.*
Player: *Have you got one with black hair? And a red trouser suit?*
Partner: *We've got her with red or black hair. The clothes are over there.*

Excuse me squares

1. You have lost your wallet/purse somewhere in the store.

Player: *Excuse me, I've lost my purse*
Partner: *Could you describe it?*
Player: *It's red leather.*
Partner: *And what was inside?*
Player: *My cheque card, not much cash, my driving licence …*
Partner: *Could I have your name and address, please?*

2. You want to change something you bought yesterday.

Player: *Excuse me. I bought this yesterday. It's a bit tight. Can I change it for the next size?*
Partner: *Have you got the receipt, please?*
Player: *Yes, er, here you are.*

The Department Store Game

4th floor
CDs/Videos
Computer shop
Electrical goods
Lost property
Toilets

3rd floor
Soft furnishings
Sports wear & equipment
Menswear
Hair salon

2nd floor
Young fashion
Levis shop
Toys
Books
Travel shop

1st floor
Mother & child
Ladies' wear
Knitwear
Leather goods
Accessories

Ground floor
Toiletries
Jewellery
Newsagent
Stationery
Cashpoint

Basement
Food hall
Confectionery
Household goods
Shoe repairs
Photo shop

THE ROOFTOP RESTAURANT

You have bought at least six of the items on your shopping list. Just time for a quick lunch before you have to leave for the airport!

FINISH

START

The Department Store Game · Board

17

Shopping List 3

set of darts
peppermints (strong!)
Barbie doll (latest)
CD of Irish music
raincoat
Cheddar cheese
T-shirt (Union Jack)
necklace for baby
2 presents for …

Shopping List 6

video of British or American film
English soap
jacket
marmalade
CD of Scottish music
postcards
cookery book
silk shirt
2 presents for …

Shopping List 2

CD of Welsh songs
wedding present for niece
film (slides)
shaver
magazine to read on the plane
pullover
silk tie
earrings
2 presents for …

Shopping List 5

English newspaper
computer game (for nephew)
London guide book
tin of toffees
scarf
Earl Grey tea
denim jacket
tennis racket
2 presents for …

Shopping List 1

something for a baby
box of chocolates
book for child (6)
shortbread biscuits
video (Changing of the Guard)
aftershave
handbag
sweatshirt
2 presents for …

Shopping List 4

CD of English folk songs
teddy-bear
3 pairs of socks
tea set
English dictionary
Swatch (latest)
lady's kilt
set of golf balls
2 presents for …

You have lost your purse/wallet somewhere in the store.	Your watch has stopped. Ask someone the time.	You need some stamps for your postcards.
You need some money.	You want to change something you bought yesterday.	You need the toilet.
You bought something yesterday that isn't working properly.	You left something to be repaired. Collect it.	Arrange to have something sent to your country.
Ask a shop assistant about souvenirs.	You left something to be repaired. Ask if it is ready yet.	You have bought someone a present. Ask about a wrapping service.
You drop something on the floor. It breaks.	You don't understand British/US sizes. You would like to try on some shoes.	You have a headache. Ask where you can get something for it.
You buy a teapot. When you look in the box you find the shop assistant has given you the wrong colour.	You need to make a phone call.	You are not satisfied with the service you have been given.

The Grammar Game

a General English game

In this game learners practise their grammar.

Language

Level
from lower intermediate

Grammar
- adverbs of frequency: *always, never, often, sometimes, usually*
- *all, both, each other*
- comparison: *than, as ... as, not as ... as*
- future forms: *going to, will*
- *if* vs. *when*
- modal verbs: *can, could, (don't) have to, may, might, must, mustn't, should*
- passive form: *is/are (done), has/have been (done), will be (done)*
- past tenses: *last week, yesterday, ago, already, ever, just, since, yet, still*
- prepositions of time: *until, by*
- Present progressive: *at the moment*
- quantifiers: *some, any, much, many, a lot, a little, a few*
- question words: *how, what, when, where, which, who*
- *so, such*

Preparation

Before the lesson
Look at the cards on pages 22–24. These contain the items in the list above and should enable learners to produce a number of useful sentences in combination with the pictures on the board (see **How to play**).

However you may prefer to use the blank cards on page 112 to give your learners a different selection or to test other items that you have been teaching recently.

You will need
- one A3-size photocopy of the board on page 21 per group 4–6 learners;
- one cut-up set of the cards on pages 22–24 (or your own cards) per group;
- one dice per group;
- one marker per player.

The Game

Introduction
Divide learners into groups of 4–6 players. Give each group a board, dice, markers and a set of cards.

Ask learners to gather round one board. Place the cards face down on the board. Demonstrate the game by making a move and eliciting a sentence connecting one of the pictures with one of the cards.

The aim of the game
The winner is the first player to reach FINISH. You may wish to set a time limit rather than wait for a player to reach the final square. The winner is then the player who has made the most moves.

How to play
Players place their markers on START. The first player to throw a 6 begins. Players take it in turns to throw the dice and move around the board.

Players landing on a picture square take the top card from the pack, read it out and create a sentence that connects the two convincingly. If the rest of the group approve of the sentence, the game proceeds; if not, the player returns to his or her previous position.

Key
(some examples)

Picture: Eiffel Tower
+ Card: never

= *I've never been to Paris.*

Picture: car
+ Card: going to

= *I'm going to clean my car tomorrow.*

Picture: hamburger
+ Card: a lot

= *A lot of people love hamburgers, but I don't like them very much.*

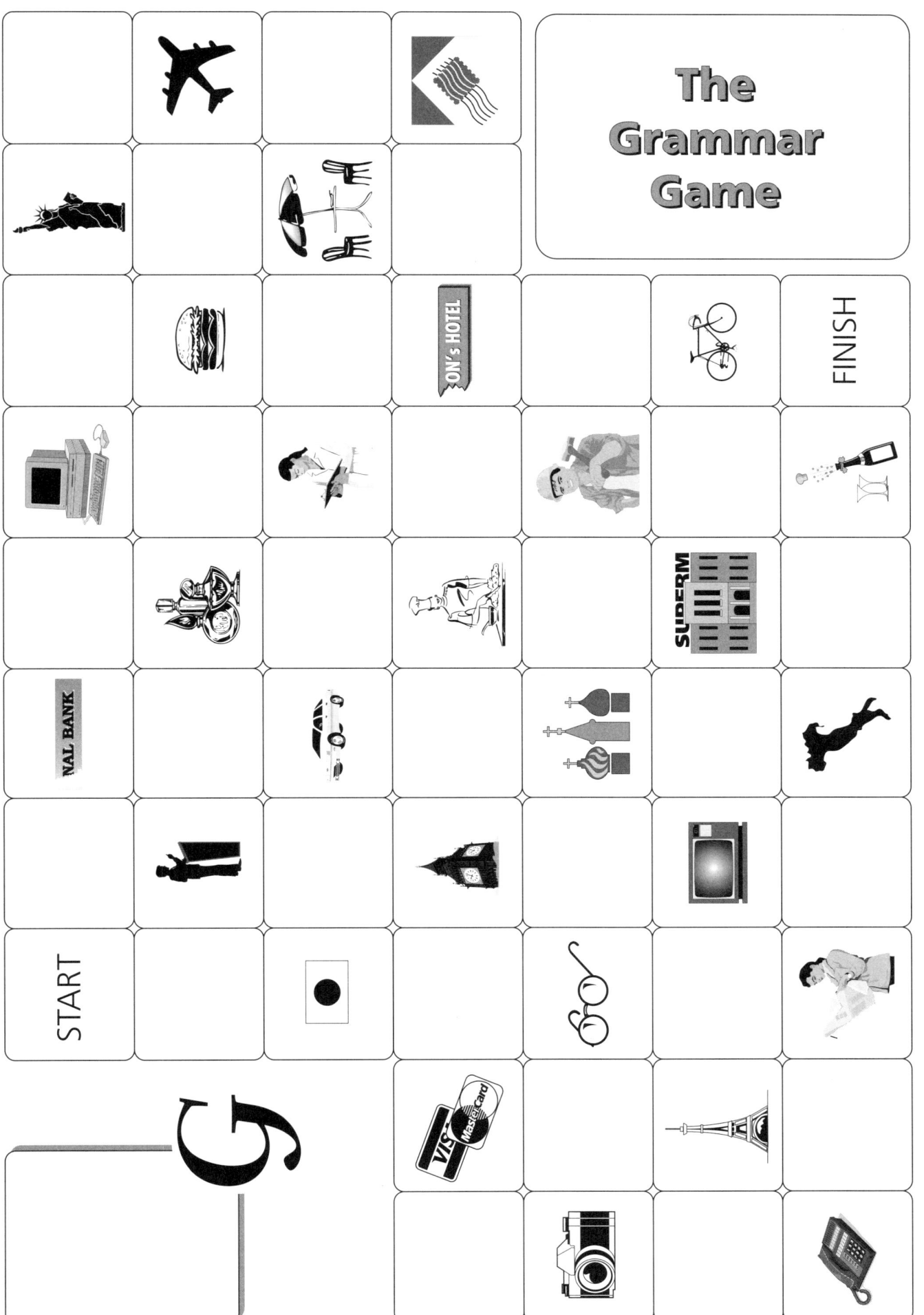

The Grammar Game

FINISH

START

at the moment	sometimes	never
always	usually	often
than	as … as	not as … as
can	could	may
might	must	mustn't
have to	don't have to	should

how	what	who
when	where	which
much	many	some
any	a lot	a little
a few	so	such
all	both	each other

The Grammar Game · Cards

until	by	if
when	is/are (done)	has/have been (done)
will be (done)	last week	yesterday
ago	already	ever
just	since	yet
still	going to	will

The Holiday Game

a General English game

In this game learners talk about holidays and associated problems.

Language

Level
from intermediate

Situations
airport, bank, car hire, hotel, illness, making small talk, restaurant, railway station

Functions
- describing people, places and objects
- expressing likes, dislikes and preferences
- expressing dissatisfaction
- giving directions
- giving opinions
- introducing oneself
- suggesting and recommending

Topics
- clothes
- holiday activities and facilities
- souvenirs
- types of holiday
- weather

Preparation

Before the lesson
This game uses 2 sets of cards: *Baggage* cards and *Oh, no!* cards. Look at the cards on pages 28–29 and decide whether you want to use them or make your own using the blank cards on page 112.

You will need
- one A3-size photocopy of the board on page 27 per group of 4–6 learners;
- one cut-up set of the cards on pages 28–29 per group;
- one dice per group;
- one marker per player.

The Game

Introduction
Divide learners into groups of 4–6 players. Give each group a board, dice, markers and sets of *Baggage* and *Oh, no!* cards.

Ask learners to gather round one board. Place the two packs of cards face down on the board. Demonstrate the game by making one or two moves and eliciting appropriate responses (see **Key** for suggestions).

The aim of the game
The winner is the first player to reach FINISH. You may wish to set a time limit rather than wait for a player to reach the final square. The winner is then the player who has made the most moves.

How to play
Players place their markers on START. The first player to throw a 6 begins. Players take it in turns to throw the dice and move around the board.

Players landing on a normal square respond to the instructions, interacting with another player where necessary. Players landing on a *Baggage* or an *Oh, no!* square take the top card from the appropriate pack and respond accordingly. If the rest of the group approve of the response, the game proceeds; if not, the player returns to his or her previous position.

Key
(some possible reponses)

1. Recommend a club-style holiday. Give reasons.
   Why don't you go to ... You'd love it – the sport facilities are fantastic – you can play tennis, golf and go diving and surfing.

2. Introduce yourself and your family or friends to someone at breakfast in your hotel.
   Good morning. My name's ... This is my ... We arrived last night.

4. You are on the beach. You can't find a friend. Describe him/her.
   I'm looking for someone. She's tall and has got blonde hair. She's about 30 and she's wearing a sort of long blue shirt ...

5. Tell a tourist about a historic building in your town.
   It was built about 500 years ago. The tower ...

6. Ask someone you meet on holiday about their work and say what you do.
   What do you do?
   I work for a small company outside X.

8. You get on a train. Ask politely about a seat, then start up a conversation.
   - *Excuse me. Is this seat free?*
   - *Do you mind if I sit here?*
   - *The countryside's lovely, isn't it?*

10. You want to hire a car. Explain what you want and give personal details.
I'd like to rent a car for a week. It's just for the two of us and we haven't got much baggage, so it can be something quite small. My name's ...

12. You are in a souvenir shop. Explain what you want and ask about prices.
I'm looking for a present for my daughter. She likes silver jewellery. Have you got any earrings? How much do these cost?

14. You are at a railway station. Ask about train times and buy a ticket.
- *Can you tell me when the next train to ... is, please?*
- *A day return, please.*

16. You are at a hotel reception. Ask about rooms and check the price.
- *I'd like a double room with a shower for two nights.*
- *How much did you say that would be?*

18. You are talking to some people you have met on holiday. Suggest somewhere to go this evening.
Let's have dinner at that restaurant near the harbour and then walk around the town and find a bar.

20. Say what you think about camping holidays.
I'm not very keen on camping holidays. I like a real bed and a proper bathroom! And what do you do if it rains?

22. You are looking at holiday photos. Describe one.
This is me and Lydia. We're in one of the bars down at the harbour drinking ouzo, as usual. I'm wearing my Greek hat.

24. You are back at your hotel after a sightseeing trip. You see some other people who were on the same trip.
- *Hello! Are you staying here as well?*
- *Did you enjoy the trip?*
- *Those mountain roads were terrible, weren't they?*

26. Talk about winter holidays.
I'd love to have a winter holiday. I don't ski, but I would like to be able to lie in the sun somewhere in the middle of winter.

28. You are unwell on holiday. Tell the doctor what the problem is.
- *I've got a pain in my stomach.*
- *My head's very hot and I feel sick.*

30. You are changing money at a bank. Say how you want it and ask about using Eurocheques.
- *Ten one hundreds please.*
- *Could you tell me if it's cheaper to use Eurocheques or a credit card?*

32. Give your opinion of package holidays.
They're OK. They're cheap and everything's organized for you.

34. Give a tourist directions to a historic site.
It's in ... street. You go down there, turn left at the lights and it's on the left. You can't miss it!

35. Compliment some of the local people on their town, village or island.
I love it here. It's one of the prettiest villages I've ever seen.

36. You are in a restaurant. Ask for the menu and then order lunch.
Could I have the menu, please?
I'll start with fish soup and then I'd like a steak – rare – and a green salad ...

38. Give your opinion of cycling holidays.
- *Fantastic! There's something new all the time, and you lose weight!*
- *Not for me! Too much hard work!*

39. Suggest a holiday for a young couple with two small children.
Why don't you go to one of those family holiday centres where they have indoor swimming pools and there's someone to look after the kids?

40. Tell some new arrivals at your hotel which sightseeing trips not to go on!
Well, there's a boat trip to ..., but it's full of tourist shops and bars playing loud music ...

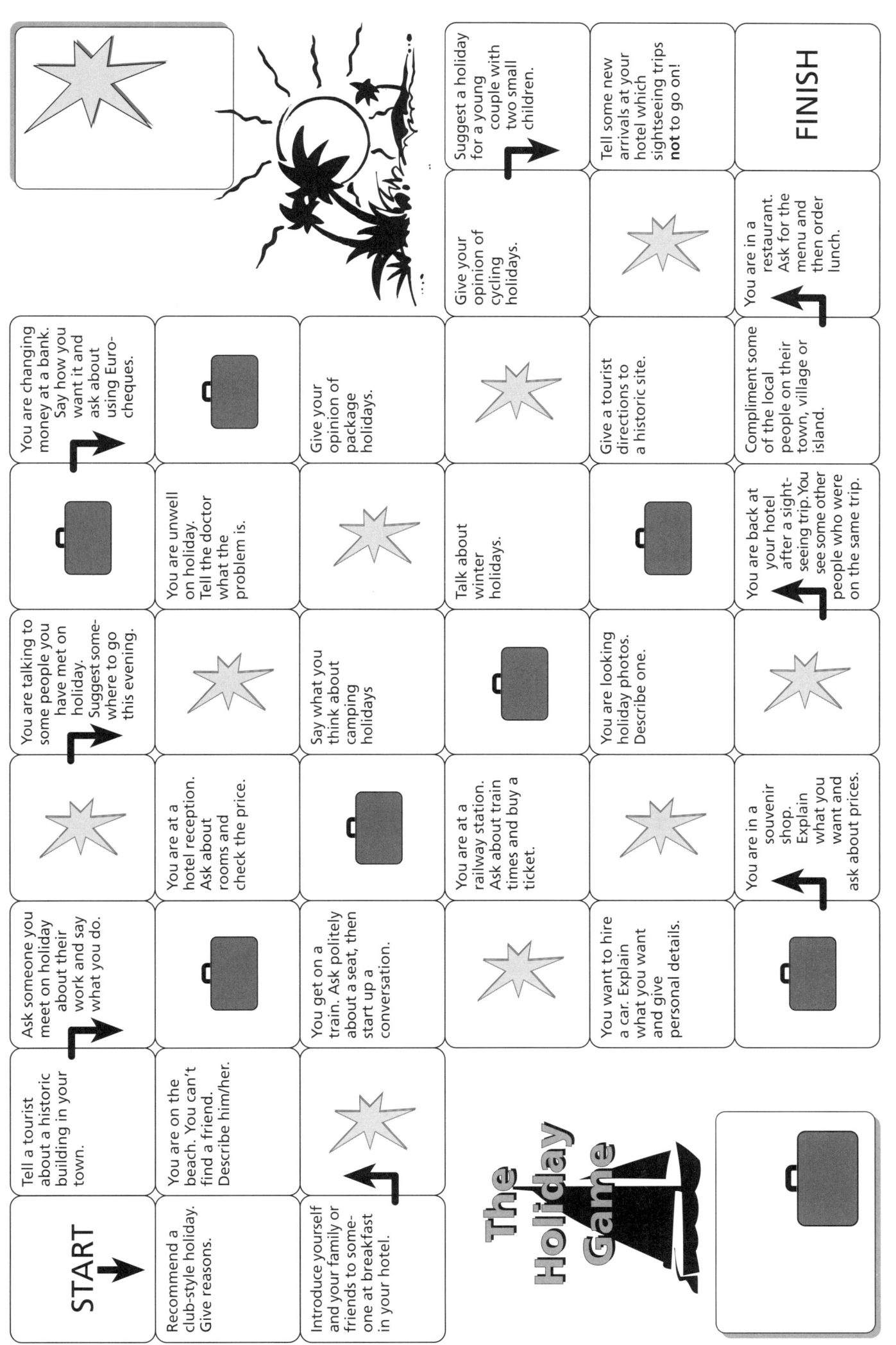

START →

Tell a tourist about a historic building in your town.

Recommend a club-style holiday. Give reasons.

You are on the beach. You can't find a friend. Describe him/her.

Introduce yourself and your family or friends to someone at breakfast in your hotel.

Ask someone you meet on holiday about their work and say what you do.

You get on a train. Ask politely about a seat, then start up a conversation.

You want to hire a car. Explain what you want and give personal details.

You are talking to some people you have met on holiday. Suggest somewhere to go this evening.

You are at a hotel reception. Ask about rooms and check the price.

Say what you think about camping holidays

You are at a railway station. Ask about train times and buy a ticket.

You are looking holiday photos. Describe one.

You are in a souvenir shop. Explain what you want and ask about prices.

You are changing money at a bank. Say how you want it and ask about Euro-cheques.

You are unwell on holiday. Tell the doctor what the problem is.

Give your opinion of package holidays.

Talk about winter holidays.

Give a tourist directions to a historic site.

You are back at your hotel after a sightseeing trip. You see some other people who were on the same trip.

Suggest a holiday for a young couple with two small children.

Tell some new arrivals at your hotel which sightseeing trips **not** to go on!

Give your opinion of cycling holidays.

You are in a restaurant. Ask for the menu and then order lunch.

Compliment some of the local people on their town, village or island.

FINISH

The Holiday Game

A young couple with a baby are going to Spain for a fortnight. They will be travelling by car and staying in an apartment. What should they pack?

A family with two teenage boys is going skiing at a famous Alpine resort. What should they pack?

A teenage girl is going to an English seaside town for two weeks to learn the language. What should she pack?

A group of ladies are off to a big city for a weekend's shopping and fun. What should they pack?

A group of four are going on a coach trip to an Eastern European city. They plan to go to the theatre and the opera. What should they pack?

A couple in their fifties are going to spend ten days walking in the Alps. It's autumn. What should they pack?

A male student wants to spend the summer vacation hitch-hiking around Europe. What should he pack?

Two couples are off to the Middle East for a beach and diving holiday over Christmas. What should they pack?

Two women are going on holiday to Kenya. They have booked a week on a photo safari and a week on the beach. What should they pack?

A couple in their sixties are flying to India, then travelling around by coach and sleeping in a trailer. What should they pack?

A young couple are going on an adventure holiday and will be spending three weeks in the Brazilian jungle. What should they pack?

Your neighbours are going to America for six weeks. They want to see as much as possible by Greyhound bus. What should they pack?

Two young women are going to Tuscany to paint. They will be staying in a farmhouse for two weeks. What should they pack?

An elderly lady is going on a ten-day Mediterranean cruise. What should she pack?

A group of men are going on a cycling holiday. They plan to be away for a week and cover about a hundred kilometres a day. What should they pack?

A group of young people are going to France for a one-week culture and gourmet holiday. What should they pack?

A group of senior citizens has booked a two-week holiday on Crete. They are interested in birds and wild flowers. What should they pack?

Where are you going on your next holiday? What will you pack?

Your flight was delayed and now you have missed your connecting flight. What next?

You are in London and your passport and plane ticket are missing. You last had them in the underground. What next?

You are on a package holiday. On arriving at your hotel, you are told that it has been overbooked. What next?

You are not satisfied with your hotel room. What next?

You planned to visit a village in the mountains today, but your partner has gone off on the wrong bus. What next?

Your hotel looked very different in the brochure. It is unfinished and at least three kilometres from the beach. What next?

You have arrived at your hotel but your baggage has not. What next?

You have been staying on a small island. All flights have been cancelled due to bad weather. What next?

You have just finished an expensive meal and realize that you don't have enough money to pay the bill. What next?

It has rained the whole first week of your summer holiday and they say next week will be the same. What next?

Your car has been broken into and your suitcases stolen. What next?

Your hotel washbasin doesn't have a plug and the shower doesn't work properly. What next?

On an excursion by boat you are terribly seasick but the only way back is also by sea. What next?

Your hotel breakfast is the same every day: bread, jam and instant coffee. What next?

You have eaten something that made you sick. What next?

You are sure that your waiter has overcharged you. What next?

You thought your flight home was tomorrow but you've just seen some other people you flew out with sitting in the airport bus. What next?

You are walking in wild country miles from the nearest village when your partner hurts an ankle. It is mid-afternoon. What next?

The Holiday Game · Cards

The People Game

a General English game

In this game learners practise talking about families, friends and famous people.

Language

Level
elementary

Topics / Vocabulary areas
- abilities
- clothes and fashion
- food and drink
- relatives
- habits, hobbies and interests
- health
- home and furnishings
- jobs
- marital status

Functions
- describing appearance and personality
- giving personal details
- talking about likes and dislikes
- expressing wishes

Preparation

Before the lesson
This game uses 4 different packs of cards: *Personal information, Family & friends, Other people* and *Stars & celebrities*. Each pack contains 9 cards. Look at the cards on pages 33–34 and decide whether you want to use them or make your own using the blank cards on page 112.

You will need
- one A3-size photocopy of the board on page 32 per group of 4 players;
- one cut-up set of the cards on pages 33–34 (or your own cards) per group;
- one dice per group;
- one marker per player.

The Game

Introduction
Divide learners into groups of 4 (one player for each corner of the board). Give each group a board, dice, markers and a full set of 36 cards.

Ask learners to gather round one board. Place the 4 packs of cards face down on the board. Demonstrate the game by making one or two moves and eliciting appropriate responses (see **Key** for suggestions).

The aim of the game
The winner is the first player to reach FINISH. You may wish to set a time limit rather than wait for a player to reach the middle of the board. The winner is then the player who has made the most moves.

How to play
Each player chooses a corner of the board and places his or her marker on START. The first player to throw a 6 begins. Players take it in turns to throw the dice and move around their corner of the board.

Players landing on a square take the top card from the appropriate pack, read it out and respond accordingly, interacting with a partner if necessary. If the rest of the group approve of the response, the game proceeds; if not, the player returns to his or her previous position.

Key
(some possible responses)

Card set 1: *Personal information*

Introduce yourself to someone else.
My name's …; I'm from …

Who do you look like?
I look like my mother. She's got black hair and brown eyes, too.

Talk about your favourite clothes.
My favourite clothes are blue jeans, T-shirts and a red pullover.

Give your name, address and telephone number.
My name's … and my address is … My telephone number is …

Talk about your hobbies.
I like …; I often play tennis …

Talk about three things you can do well.
I can draw, play the piano, speak Italian …

Talk about things you like.
I like cats, books, cooking …

Talk about your past.
- *I was born in …*
- *I lived in …*
- *I went to school in …*

What do you do when you are bored?
- *I eat a lot.*
- *I try to get some exercise.*

Card set 2: *Family & friends*

Describe someone in your family.
My daughter is 23; she's a student. She's quite tall and has got blue eyes …

Name five things in a friend's living room.
sofa, armchair, bookshelves, TV, CD player, painting

Give directions to a friend's home.
First on the right, then third on the left. It's next to the school.

Think of three friends or relatives. Say what colours they like.
My mother loves blue, my wife buys a lot of black clothes and my brother often wears red.

Talk about what one of your friends or relatives enjoyed doing as a teenager.
She sat around a lot, listening to pop music; she went to discos ...

Think of two friends or relatives. What are their hobbies?
My sister loves gardening and her husband collects stamps.

Describe a friend or relative.
He's 42 years old, tall, dark-haired and quite good-looking.

Talk about a friend's past.
She was born in England. Her parents were from Austria. She went to school in England and started work in Vienna ...

Talk about what some friends or relatives are doing right now.
Well, ...'s watching television, ...'s probably having supper ...

Card set 3: *Other people*

Think of three words that tell you someone's marital status.
single, engaged, married, divorced, separated, widow/widower

Think of five people you know. What are their jobs?
doctor, secretary, electrician, dentist, shop assistant, engineer

Describe a family you know.
There's a father, a mother, three children. The children are 9, 7 and 5, ...

Talk about what people in your area do at the weekend.
On Saturdays, most people get up a bit later than usual and then go shopping. Older people usually stay at home in the evening but young people go out to a disco or the movies. On Sundays, a lot of families ...

Describe someone's personality.
My boss is all right when she's in a good mood, but she can be very impatient when things are difficult.

What sort of things do people in your area eat?
A lot of young people seem to eat fast food, like hamburgers and pizzas.
Older couples are more traditional; they cook things like ...

Talk about fashions in your area at the moment.
Well, the girls are all wearing ...

Think of two people you've seen today. Compare them.
There were two men on the bus. One was about 25, the other was older, probably about 40. He was thinner. The younger man looked fitter ...

Compare people from your area with people from other parts of your country.
Well, people in this area are friendlier than ...

Card set 4: *Stars & celebrities*

(see cards)

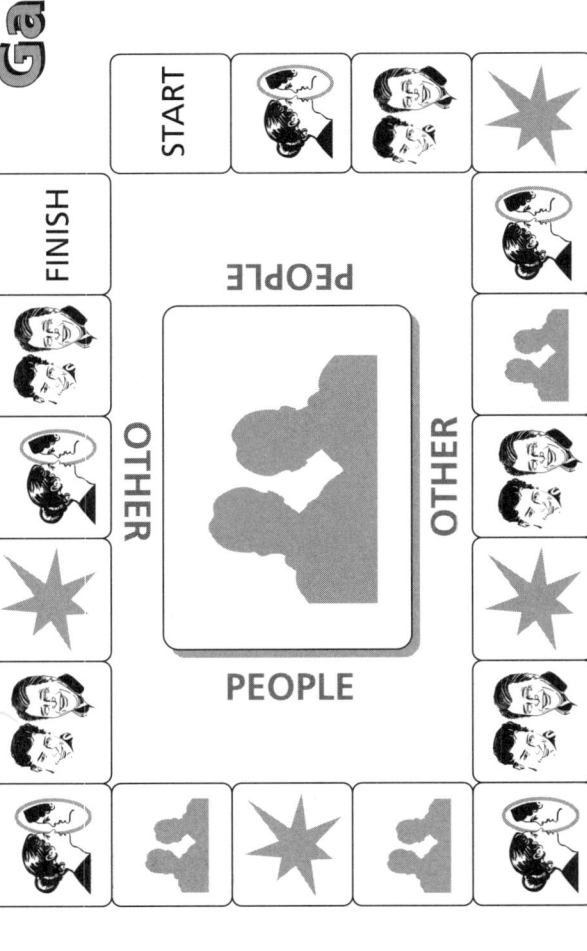

The People Game

Introduce yourself to someone else.

Who do you look like?

Talk about your favourite clothes.

Give your name, address and telephone number.

Talk about your hobbies.

Talk about three things you can do well.

Talk about things you like.

Talk about your past.

What do you do when you are bored?

Describe some one in your family.

Name five things in a friend's living room.

Give directions to a friend's home.

Think of three friends or relatives. Say what colours they like.

Talk about what one of your friends or relatives enjoyed doing as a teenager.

Think of two friends or relatives. What are their hobbies?

Describe a friend or relative.

Talk about a friend's past.

Talk about what some friends or relatives are doing right now.

Think of three words that tell you someone's marital status.

Think of five people you know. What are their jobs?

Describe a family you know.

Talk about what people in your area do at the weekend.

Describe someone's personality.

What sort of things do people in your area eat?

Talk about fashions in your area at the moment.

Think of two people you've seen today. Compare them.

Compare people from your area with people from other parts of your country.

Describe a famous sportsman or woman. The others have to say who it is.

Describe a head of state. The others have to guess who it is.

Describe a famous politician. The others have to guess who it is.

Describe a film star. The others have to guess who it is.

Describe a pop star. The others have to guess who it is.

Describe a TV personality. The others have to guess who it is.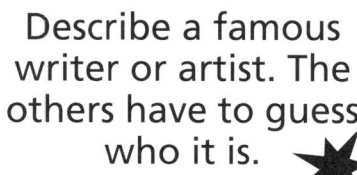

Describe a famous writer or artist. The others have to guess who it is.

Describe a local personality. The others have to guess who it is.

Describe a historical person. The others have to guess who it is.

The Politeness Game

a General English game

In this game learners practise expressing themselves politely in everyday situations.

Language

Level
from lower intermediate

Functions
- congratulating and being congratulated
- giving and receiving bad/good news
- making and accepting apologies
- making and receiving compliments
- making excuses
- making, accepting and refusing invitations
- opening and closing conversations
- talking about health
- talking about the weather

Preparation

Before the lesson
Decide whether you want to use the cards on pages 39–41 or make your own using the blank cards on page 112.

You will need
- one A3-size photocopy of the board on page 38 per group of 4–6 learners;
- one cut-up set of the cards on pages 39–41 (or your own cards) per group;
- one dice per group;
- one marker per player.

The Game

Introduction
Divide learners into groups of 4–6 players. Give each group a board, dice, markers and a set of cards.

Ask learners to gather round one board. Place the cards face down on the board. Demonstrate the game by making one or two moves and eliciting appropriate responses (see **Key** for suggestions).

The aim of the game
The winner is the first player to reach FINISH. You may wish to set a time limit rather than wait for a player to reach the final square. The winner is then the player who has made the most moves.

How to play
Players place their markers on START. The first player to throw a 6 begins. Players take it in turns to throw the dice and move around the board.

Players landing on a square take the top card from the pack, read it out and respond accordingly, interacting with a partner if necessary. If the rest of the group approve of the response, the game proceeds; if not, the player returns to his or her previous position.

Key
(some possible responses)

Someone sneezes. What do you say?
Bless you!

You're just going to start eating. What do you say?
- *Bon appetit.*
- *Enjoy your meal!*
- *(nothing)*

You need the salt. It's at the other end of the table. What do you say?
Could you pass the salt, please?

You tread on someone's foot. What do you say?
- *Sorry! / I'm so sorry. (UK)*
- *Pardon me! / Excuse me! (US)*

You see there's a bee in someone's glass. What do you say?
Watch out! / Be careful! There's a bee in your glass!

A friend has just had a baby. What do you say?
Congratulations!

Greet a friend on December 25th.
- *Merry Christmas!*
- *Happy Christmas!*

It's a friend's birthday. What do you say?
- *Happy birthday!*
- *Many happy returns!*

Someone congratulates you on your birthday. What do you say?
Thank you!

A friend is leaving for the airport. What do you say?
Have a good flight/trip/holiday!

You've just finished chatting to a friend. What do you say?
- *Bye, see you soon!*
- *See you later.*

Someone thanks you for something – unnecessarily. What do you say?
- *That's OK.*
- *Don't mention it.*
- *You're welcome.*

A friend can't come to dinner. What do you say?
What a pity! Maybe next time.

A friend offers to give you a lift home. What do you say?
- *That would be nice, thank you.*
- *That's very kind of you.*

You and a friend are going to the same exhibition. You don't have a car. What do you say?
Could you give me a lift (US: ride), please?

An acquaintance says, "Give my regards to ... ." What do you say?
Yes, of course.

Someone asks you – a non-smoker – for a light. What do you say?
Sorry, I don't smoke.

Comment on the weather.
A bit cold today, isn't it?

A friend says, "Lovely day today, isn't it?" What do you say?
Yes, lovely/beautiful!

Someone pushes in front of you in a queue. What do you say?
Excuse me, I think I was next.

A colleague gives you a birthday present. What do you say?
- *That's very kind of you!*
- *You really shouldn't have!*

Greet someone in the morning.
- *Good morning.*
- *Hello, how are you?*

A friend says, "Morning, how are you?" What do you say?
- *Fine, thanks.*
- *Not too bad, thanks*

(Note that this is not really a question about your health, unless you are speaking to a close friend.)

You want someone to pass your greetings on to another person. What do you say?
- *Remember me to ...*
- *Give my regards to ...*

Someone says, "Merry Christmas!" What do you say?
Thank you! The same to you.

It's freezing cold and snowing hard. What do you say?
Terrible weather today, isn't it?

Mention a health problem to a close friend who asks you how you are.
Well, I've got a very bad cold and I didn't sleep at all last night ...

Say goodbye to an old friend you have just met again.
Well, it was nice/lovely to see you again; we must meet more often.

A woman asks you to help her with a heavy push-chair. You have back problems. What do you say?
I'm very sorry, but I'm afraid I can't lift heavy things.

You've forgotten your purse/wallet. Ask a friend to help you.
I can't find my purse. Could you possibly lend me ...

A friend forgot to post a letter. What do you say?
Never mind, you can do it tomorrow ...

You are sitting in a draught. What do you say?
May I / Do you mind if I close the window?

Someone asks you a very personal question. What do you say?
I'd rather not answer that, if you don't mind.

A child is going to cross the road. You see a car is coming. What do you say?
Mind out!

Comment on someone's new shirt.
- *What a lovely shirt!*
- *I do like your shirt.*

Refuse an invitation politely.
I'd love to come, but I'm afraid I have to ...

Start a conversation with someone on a flight or train journey.
- *The food is really good, isn't it?*
- *This train's very crowded, isn't it?*
- *It's very warm in here, isn't it?*

You have unintentionally gone to the front of a queue. What do you say?
Oh, I'm sorry! I didn't realize ...

Finish a conversation with a friend who is ill.
- *I hope you feel better soon.*
- *Take care of yourself.*

A friend has put on a piece of clothing wrongly. What do you say?
- *Er ... your pullover's back to front/ inside out.*
- *You've buttoned up your shirt the wrong way.*

Thank someone for inviting you round for supper.
Thank you. That was very nice. It's been a lovely evening.

Ask someone a favour.
- *Do you think you could ...*
- *I hope you don't mind me asking, but ...*

You have a heavy suitcase which has to go in the luggage rack. What do you say?
- *Excuse me, could you help me ...*
- *Would you mind helping me ...*

You have a low car. Your friend is tall and is just about to get in. What do you say?
Mind your head!

There's only one empty seat in the train. What do you say?
• *Excuse me, is anyone sitting here?*
• *Is this seat free/taken?*

At lunch in the canteen a colleague says, "May I join you?". What do you say?
• *Yes, of course.*
• *Please do.*

You want to call a waiter. What do you say?
Excuse me!

You push someone in a crowded shop. What do you say?
• *Sorry. (UK)*
• *Pardon me. / Excuse me. (US)*

Someone has just passed their driving test. What do you say?
• *Well done!*
• *Congratulations!*

You want to get past someone. What do you say?
Excuse me.

Someone asks you the way. You're new in town. What do you say?
Sorry, I'm a stranger here myself.

Someone pays you a compliment. What do you say?
Oh, thank you!

Say something nice about someone's pullover.
What a lovely ...

A friend breaks one of your best glasses. What do you say?
• *Don't worry.*
• *It doesn't matter.*

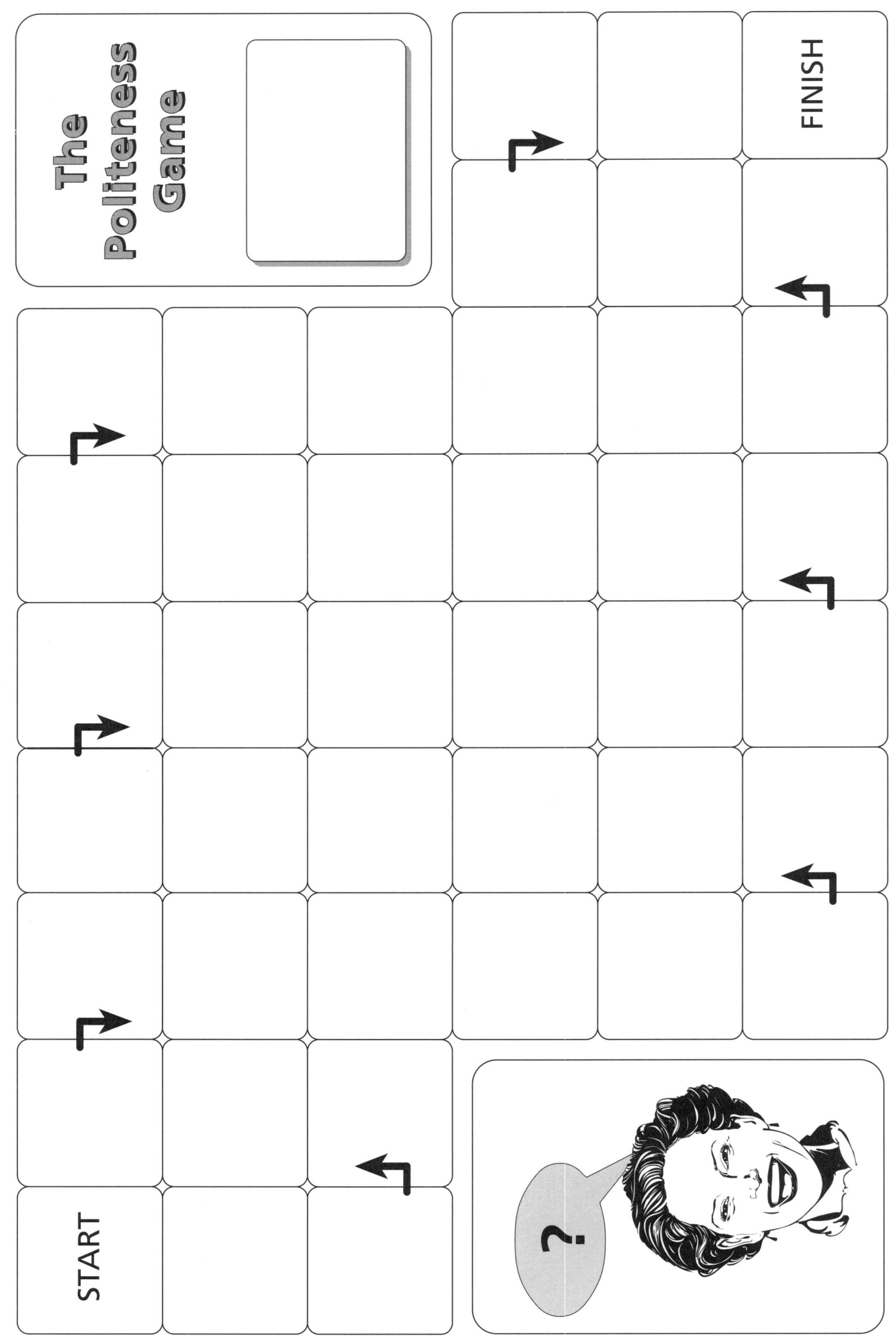

The Politeness Game

START

FINISH

?

Someone sneezes. What do you say?

You're just going to start eating. What do you say?

You need the salt. It's at the other end of the table. What do you say?

You tread on someone's foot. What do you say?

You see there's a bee in someone's glass. What do you say?

A friend has just had a baby. What do you say?

Greet a friend on December 25th.

It's a friend's birthday. What do you say?

Someone congratulates you on your birthday. What do you say?

A friend is leaving for the airport. What do you say?

You've just finished chatting to a friend. What do you say?

Someone thanks you for something – unnecessarily. What do you say?

A friend can't come to dinner. What do you say?

A friend offers to give you a lift home. What do you say?

You and a friend are going to the same exhibition. You don't have a car. What do you say?

An acquaintance says, "Give my regards to …" What do you say?

Someone asks you – a non-smoker – for a light. What do you say?

Comment on the weather.

The Politeness Game · Cards

A friend says, "Lovely day today, isn't it?" What do you say?

Someone pushes in front of you in a queue. What do you say?

A colleague gives you a birthday present. What do you say?

Greet someone in the morning.

A friend says, "Morning, how are you?" What do you say?

You want someone to pass your greetings on to another person. What do you say?

Someone says, "Merry Christmas." What do you say?

It's freezing cold and snowing hard. What do you say?

Mention a health problem to a close friend who asks you how you are.

Say goodbye to an old friend you have just met again.

A woman asks you to help her with a heavy pushchair. You have back problems. What do you say?

You've forgotten your purse/wallet. Ask a friend to help you.

A friend forgot to post a letter. What do you say?

You are sitting in a draught. What do you say?

Someone asks you a very personal question. What do you say?

A child is going to cross the road. You see a car is coming. What do you say?

Comment on someone's new shirt.

Refuse an invitation politely.

Start a conversation with someone on a flight or train journey.

You have unintentionally gone to the front of a queue. What do you say?

Finish a conversation with a friend who is ill.

A friend has put on a piece of clothing wrongly. What do you say?

Thank someone for inviting you round for supper.

Ask someone a favour.

You have a heavy suitcase which has to go in the luggage rack. What do you say?

You have a low car. Your friend is tall and is just about to get in. What do you say?

There's only one empty seat in the train. What do you say?

At lunch in the canteen a colleague says, "May I join you?" What do you say?

You want to call a waiter. What do you say?

You push some-one in a crowded shop. What do you say?

Someone has just passed their driving test. What do you say?

You want to get past someone. What do you say?

Someone asks you the way. You're new in town. What do you say?

Someone pays you a compliment. What do you say?

Say something nice about someone's pullover.

A friend breaks one of your best glasses. What do you say?

The Politeness Game · Cards

The Sports Game

a General English game

In this game learners talk about various aspects of sport.

Language

Level
from intermediate

Functions
- explaining the rules of a sport
- giving opinions
- stating likes, dislikes and preferences

Topics
- indoor and outdoor sports
- local and national sport
- problems in sport (e.g. doping, hooliganism)
- seasonal sports
- sports accidents
- sports personalities
- sportswear and equipment

Preparation

Before the lesson
This game uses two sets of cards: *Track* cards and *Whistle* cards. Look at the cards on pages 44–46 and decide whether you want to use them or make your own using the blank cards on page 112.

You will need
- one A3-size photocopy of the board on page 43 per group of 4–6 learners;
- one cut-up set of the cards on pages 44–46 (or your own cards) per group;
- one dice per group;
- two markers per group.

The Game

Introduction
Divide learners into groups of 4–6 players. Give each group a board, dice, markers and sets of *Track* and *Whistle* cards. Each group then divides into two teams.

Ask learners to gather round one board. Place the two packs of cards face down on the board. Demonstrate the game by taking one or two cards and eliciting suitable responses from learners.

The aim of the game
The winners are the first team to reach FINISH. You may wish to set a time limit rather than wait for a team to cross the line. The winners are then the team that have made the most moves.

How to play
The teams place their markers on START. The first team to throw a 6 begins. Teams take it in turns to throw the dice and move around the board.

A team landing on a square picks up a *Track* card (if the square is blank) or *Whistle* card (if it contains the hand/card symbol), reads the card out and carries out the task without repeating what has already been said by others. If the other team approves, the game proceeds. If not, the team returns to its previous position.

Key
(some examples)

Name 2 international tennis tournaments.
Wimbledon, US Open, French Open (Roland Garos)

Name 2 cities which have hosted the Olympic Games.
Moscow (1980), Los Angeles (1984), Seoul (1988), Barcelona (1992), Atlanta (1996)

Name 5 ball sports.
football, rugby, basketball, volleyball, tennis, golf, billiards

Name 2 internationally-known football teams.
Ajax, Bayern München, Juventus, Liverpool, Real Madrid

"Time to go in, Your Lordship. That's the third hang-glider you've shot down."

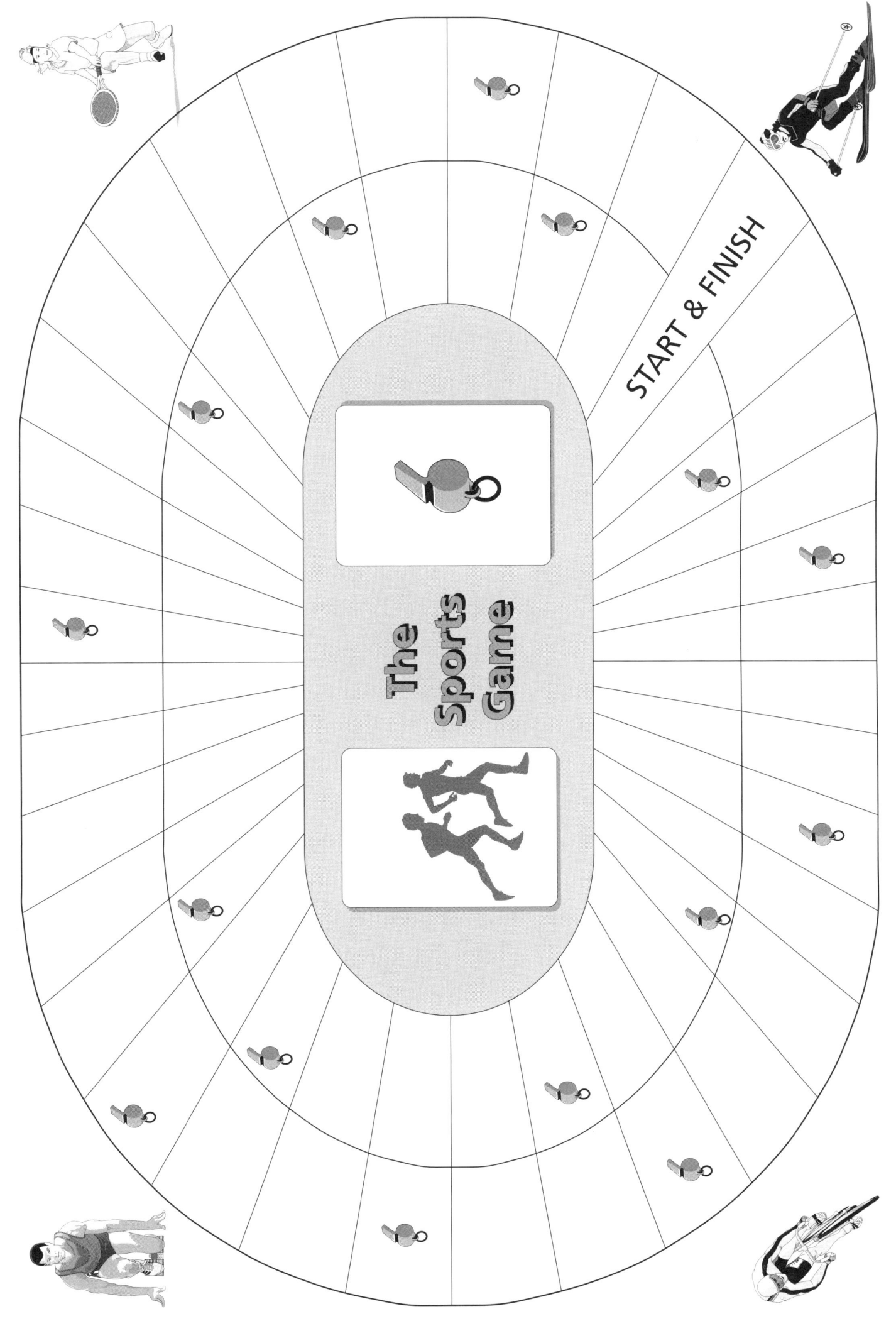

START & FINISH

The Sports Game

The Sports Game · Board   43

Talk about a
sport you
play.

Talk about a
sport you would
like to try.

Talk about an
individual
sport.

Talk about
a team
sport.

Talk about
an indoor
sport.

Talk about
a winter
sport.

Talk about the
strangest sport
you've heard
of.

Talk about
an exclusive
sport.

Talk about the
most exciting sport
you've watched in
person.

Talk about
sport and
politics.

Talk about
sport at
school.

Talk about older
people and
sport.

Talk about
sports for the
family.

Talk about sports
for handicapped
people.

Talk about
sports clubs.

Talk about a
sportswoman
you admire.

Talk about a
sportsman from
a different
country.

Talk about a
local sports
personality.

Talk about a local sports team.

Talk about a regional sport.

Talk about the benefits of sports sponsorship.

Talk about sport in the press.

Talk about sport on TV.

Talk about clothes for an outdoor sport.

Talk about sports equipment.

Talk about sport and fashion.

Talk about the benefits of the Olympic Games.

Name a new sport star.

Name a retired sport star.

Name a sport that does not require any equipment.

Name a sport that is not often played in your country.

Name 2 international tennis tournaments.

Name 2 cities which have hosted the Olympic Games.

Name 5 ball sports.

Name 2 internationally-known football teams.

Describe the rules of an international sport. The other players have to guess which sport it is.

Talk about a sport scandal.

Talk about sport stars' incomes.

Talk about a sports accident you have heard of.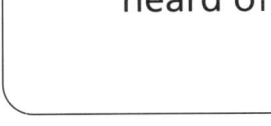

Talk about sports injuries. Who should pay for them?

Talk about sport and hooliganism.

Talk about doping and sport.

Talk about a sportswoman you do not admire.

Talk about a sportsman you do not admire.

Talk about a sport you think should be banned.

Talk about animals and sport in your country.

Talk about an unsuccessful or unlucky sportsperson.

Talk about the problems of children and sport.

Talk about winter sports and the environment.

Talk about water sports and the environment.

Talk about animals and sport in other countries.

Talk about the negative aspects of sports sponsorship.

Talk about the most boring sport you know.

Talk about a dangerous sport.

The Tenses Game

a General English game

In this game learners practise tenses.

Language

Level
from lower intermediate

Tenses
- Present simple and progressive
- Past simple and progressive
- Present perfect simple and progressive
- Present and Past simple passive
- Past perfect
- Future reference (*will, going to* and Present progressive as future)

Preparation

Before the lesson
Decide whether you want to use the cards on pages 51–53. The game can be simplified by taking out any cards that require more complicated tenses. Alternatively, make your own cards using the blank cards on page 112.

You will need
- one A3-size photocopy of the board on page 50 per group of 4–6 learners;
- one cut-up set of the cards on pages 51–53 (or your own cards) per group;
- one dice per group;
- one marker per player.

The Game

Introduction
Divide learners into groups of 4–6 players. Give each group a board, dice, markers and a set of cards.

Ask learners to gather round one board. Place the cards face down on the board. Demonstrate the game by making one or two moves and eliciting appropriate responses (see **Key** for suggestions).

The aim of the game
The winner is the first player to a) gain 50 points and then b) throw a 6 to get off the board (in any direction).

How to play
Players place their markers in the middle of the board. The first player to throw a 6 begins. Players take it in turns to throw the dice and move vertically or horizontally in any direction.

Players landing on a patterned circle take the top card from the pack, read it out and respond accordingly, producing at least one complete sentence. If the rest of the group approve of the response, the player gains points according to the pattern of the circle they are on (see the board).

Players landing on a blank circle may not pick up a card.

Key
(some possible responses)

Talk about when you get up and what you have for breakfast.
I get up at … every day . I have a cup of coffee with some toast and marmalade.

Talk about a typical weekday.
I start work at … I usually have lunch in the company canteen …

Say how you go to work.
By train. I leave home at … and walk to the station. I catch the … train to …

Talk about the climate in your country.
It rains a lot in spring. The winters are usually very cold and it snows a lot.

How often do you go to the dentist and to the hairdresser's?
I go to the dentist every six months and the hairdresser's every two months.

Talk about an average family who live in your area.
They have two children. They live in a flat, they have two cars and spend their holidays in Italy.

Ask someone about their likes and dislikes.
What do you like? What don't you like?

Give three pieces of information about one of your friends, relatives or colleagues.
My cousin lives in … He works for a bank … In his free time, he …

Think of a friend, relative or colleague. What do you think he or she is doing now?
She's probably sitting in her living room and watching television …

Make two sentences using some of these words: working / staying / travelling / cooking.
- *At the moment I'm working on a new project called …*
- *My husband likes travelling, but I prefer …*

Talk about a trend, like this:
"These days, more and more people are … ing."
These days, more and more people are travelling abroad …

Describe the weather today.
The sun's shining and it's quite hot.

What did you do yesterday evening?
I went to the cinema with some friends and then we had a meal at the …

Ask someone about last weekend.
- *What did you do last weekend?*
- *Did you … last weekend?*

What did you like best about school?
I liked … because …

Talk about something that happened in your country last month.
It rained a lot and there was a bad accident …

Talk about your last holiday.
I went to … and visited …

Complete this sentence: "Fifty years ago …"
… people didn't have computers.

Complete this sentence: "When I was a child …"
… I lived in a small village and …

Talk about a famous person who died this century.
… was an American film star. One of her films …

Talk about a favourite toy.
- *At the moment my son's favourite toy is …*
- *I had a large teddy bear when I was very small …*

Complete these two sentences:
She didn't ask you, … she?
He wasn't there, … he?
did; was

What were you doing around eight o'clock last night?
I was having supper.

You've just seen a traffic accident. Tell a police officer about it.
The red car was coming from the left. It was going very fast and the driver didn't see …

Complete this sentence and tell the story:
"An interesting thing happened to me once while I was …ing."
(personalized answer)

Look: have – had – had
Now do the same with these verbs: cost, let, put.
cost – cost – cost; let – let – let; put – put– put

Look: have – had – had
Now do the same with these verbs: bring, catch, think.
bring – brought – brought
catch – caught – caught
think – thought – thought

Look: have – had – had
Now do the same with these verbs: be, go.
be – was/were – been
go – went – been/gone

Tell the other players something that you have done but they probably haven't.
I've been to Chile.
(So have I!)
OK. I've seen the Queen of England.

What has changed in your town or area in the last few years?
- *They've built a …*
- *The … has changed quite a lot. It used to be …*

Have you ever eaten any unusual food? Talk about it.
Yes, I have. When I was in China a few years ago I had to …

Have you ever read an English book?
- *Yes, I have. I read a book of short stories …*
- *No, never.*

Talk about one way your life has changed in the last few years.
I've changed my job, I've moved …

Make a true sentence with:
"since last year".
- *I've been living here since last year.*
- *My daughter has been abroad twice since last year.*

Make a true sentence with:
"for more than five years".
- *I have lived at my present address for more than five years.*
- *I worked in … for more than five years.*

Somebody asks you: "Have you had a busy day?" What do you answer?
- *Yes, I've been working hard all day! I've cleaned the windows, washed …*
- *No, not really. It was quiet at the office today.*

Ask someone a question with this word:
ever.
- *Do you ever …*
- *Have you ever …?*

Make a sentence with these words:
not … yet.
I haven't been to the States yet, but I'd like to.

Talk about yesterday starting with these words:
"After I had finished …"
After I had finished breakfast, I got dressed and went to work.

Talk about some holiday plans.
- *I'm going to visit …*
- *My daughter and son-in-law are flying to … tomorrow.*

Talk about something you plan to buy.
I'm going to buy a new car soon.

What are you going to eat this evening?
- *We're going to have …*
- *I'm going to cook …*

Ask someone about their plans for the rest of the day.
What are you going to do this afternoon/evening?

Tell somebody about your plans for next week.
I'm going to the cinema on Monday, playing tennis on Friday …

You work too hard but want to change this. Talk about your plans.
I'm going to do more sport and find time for some hobbies.

Your child wants you to play football but the sky looks very dark. Explain why you can't at the moment.
I think it's going to rain. Let's wait a bit and see.

What changes will there be in your country in the next couple of years?
- *There'll be a new president.*
- *There'll probably be more protests about …*

What will your town probably be like in twenty years?
- *There will be even more traffic. It will be impossible to park in town.*
- *Some of the older houses will probably be gone.*

Complete this sentence:
"Our grandchildren will probably be able to …"
- *… do almost everything they want to by computer: shopping, booking …*
- *… spend their holidays on the moon …*

Complete this sentence:
"Our grandchildren will probably have to …"
- *… be more careful with water than we are.*
- *… pay more for transport than we do.*

Think of a country for the other players to guess. Give them clues using: grown / made / produced. (e.g. "A lot of coffee is grown there.").
- *Some of the best wine in the world is produced there.*
- *This is where most of the world's most successful films are made.*

Make a sentence using one of these words: designed / discovered / invented (by/in).
- *The first car was invented by Daimler.*
- *America was (not) discovered in 1492.*

Make a sentence using one of these words: painted / sung / written (by/in). (e.g. "Hamlet was written by Shakespeare.").
- *The "Mona Lisa" was painted by Leonardo da Vinci.*
- *"Yesterday" was sung by Paul McCartney.*

Think of a film for the other players to guess. Give some clues like this:
"A man was found dead in his bedroom. His wife was arrested …"
(personalized clues)

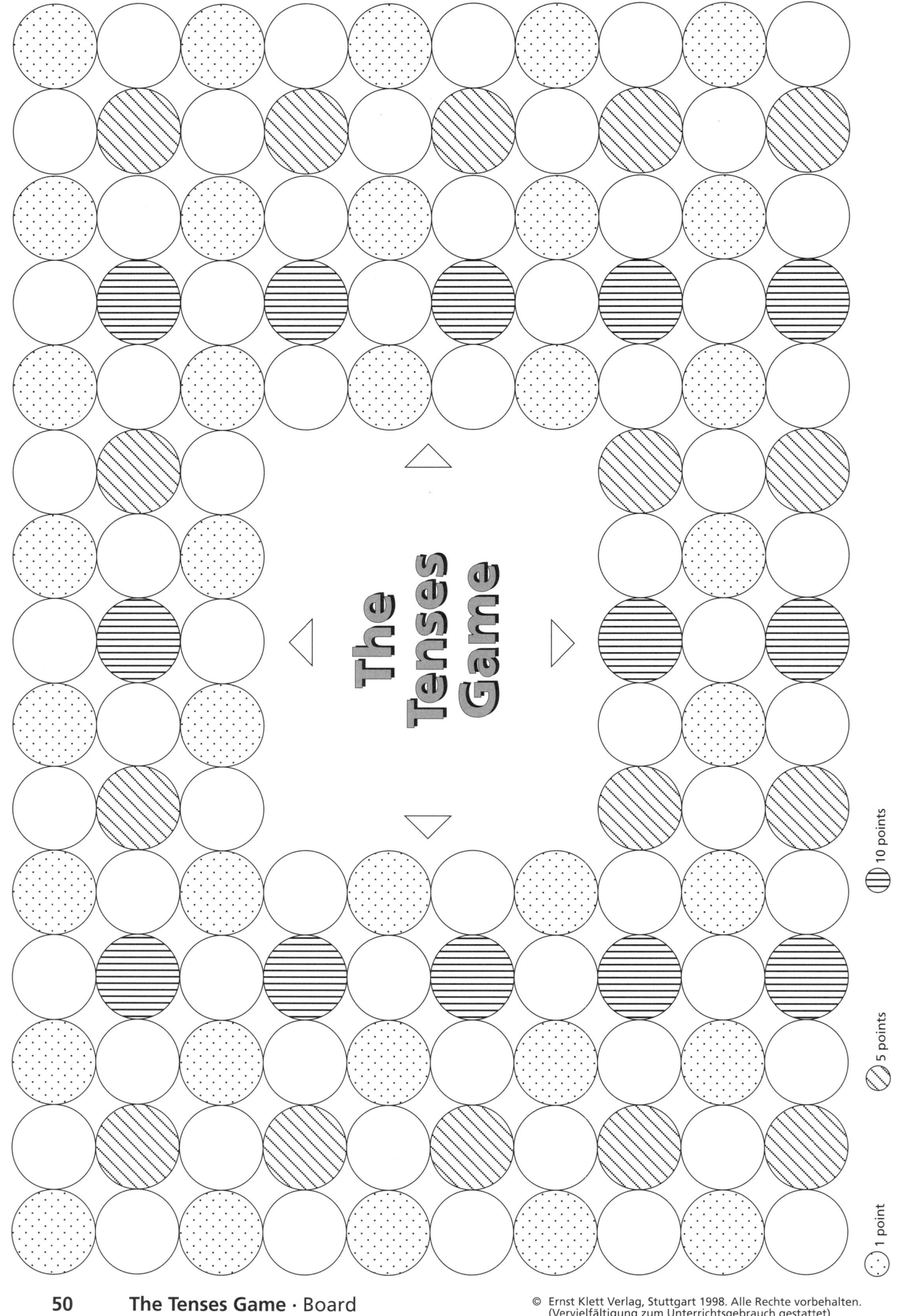

The Tenses Game

10 points

5 points

1 point

Talk about when you get up and what you have for breakfast.

Talk about a typical weekday.

Say how you go to work.

Talk about the climate in your country.

How often do you go to the dentist and to the hairdresser's?

Talk about an average family who live in your area.

Ask someone about their likes and dislikes.

Give three pieces of information about one of your friends, relatives or colleagues.

Think of a friend, relative or collea-gue. What do you think he or she is doing now?

Make two sentences using some of these words: working / staying / travelling / cooking.

Talk about a trend, like this: "These days, more and more people are …ing."

Describe the weather today.

What did you do yesterday evening?

Ask someone about last weekend.

What did you like best about school?

Talk about some-thing that happened in your country last month.

Talk about your last holiday.

Complete this sentence: "Fifty years ago …"

Complete this sentence: "When I was a child …"

Talk about a famous person who died this century.

Talk about a favourite toy.

Complete these two sentences: She didn't ask you, … she? He wasn't there, … he?

What were you doing around eight o'clock last night?

You've just seen a traffic accident. Tell a police officer about it.

Complete this sentence and tell the story: "An interesting thing happened to me once while I was …ing."

Look: have – had – had. Now do the same with these verbs: cost, let, put.

Look: have – had – had. Now do the same with these verbs: bring, catch, think.

Look: have – had – had. Now do the same with these verbs: be, go.

Tell the other players something that you have done but they probably haven't.

What has changed in your town or area in the last few years?

Have you ever eaten any unusual food? Talk about it.

Have you ever read an English book?

Talk about one way your life has changed in the last few years.

Make a true sentence with: "since last year".

Make a true sentence with: "for more than five years".

Somebody asks you: "Have you had a busy day?" What do you answer?

Ask someone a question with this word: ever.	Make a sentence with these words: not … yet.	Talk about yesterday starting with these words: "After I had finished …"
Talk about some holiday plans.	Talk about something you plan to buy.	What are you are going to eat this evening?
Ask someone about their plans for the rest of the day.	Tell somebody about your plans for next week.	You work too hard but want to change this. Talk about your plans.
Your child wants you to play football but the sky looks very dark. Explain why you can't at the moment.	What changes will there be in your country in the next couple of years?	What will your town probably be like in twenty years?
Complete this sentence: "Our grandchildren will probably be able to …"	Complete this sentence: "Our grandchildren will probably have to …"	Think of a country for the other players to guess. Give them clues using: grown/made/produced (e.g. "A lot of coffee is grown there.").
Make a sentence using one of these words: designed/discovered/ invented (by/in)	Make a sentence using one of these words: painted/sung/written (by/in) (e.g. "Hamlet was written by Shakespeare.")	Think of a film for the other players to guess. Give some clues like this: "A man was found dead in his bedroom. His wife was arrested …"

The Vocabulary Game

a General English game

In this game learners recycle their vocabulary.

Language

Level
any level

Vocabulary
Any vocabulary that you want your learners to revise.

Preparation

Before the lesson
Look at the cards on pages 56–58. These contain some low-level vocabulary from the fields of *family, food, home, travel, weather* and *leisure,* and are given to show how the game is played. You will probably want to make your own selection of vocabulary that your learners have been working on recently, using the blank cards on page 112.

You will need
- one A3-size photocopy of the board on page 55 per group of 4 learners;
- one cut-up set of the cards on pages 56–58 (or your own cards) per group;
- one dice per group;
- one marker per player.

The Game

Introduction
Divide learners into groups of 4 players. Give each group a board, dice, markers and a set of cards.

Ask learners to gather round one board. Place the cards face down on the board. Demonstrate the game by making one or two moves and eliciting appropriate responses.

The aim of the game
The winner is the first player to reach FINISH. You may wish to set a time limit rather than wait for a player to reach the final square. The winner is then the player who has made the most moves.

How to play
Players place their markers on START. The first player to throw a 6 begins. Players take it in turns to throw the dice and move around the board.

Players landing on a square take the top card from the pack and respond according to the instruction on the square. If the rest of the group approve of the response, the game proceeds; if not, the player returns to his or her previous position.

Key

(some examples)

Definition
Learner gives a definition of the word on the card, e.g. *This word means …*

Synonym or Opposite
Learner thinks of a synonym or opposite for the word on the card, e.g. *single – unmarried* or *single – married.*

(N.B. It may not always be possible to find a synonym or opposite, in which case learners have to pass.)

Word field
Learners think of at least two other words in the same word field as the word on the card, e.g. *fridge – washing machine – dishwasher.*

Word partnership
Learner thinks of a partnership for the word on the card, e.g. *music – to listen to music.*

The Vocabulary Game

START

WORD PARTNERSHIP

DEFINITION

WORD FIELD

SYNONYM OR OPPOSITE

WORD PARTNERSHIP

SYNONYM OR OPPOSITE

DEFINITION

WORD PARTNERSHIP

WORD FIELD

DEFINITION

WORD FIELD

SYNONYM OR OPPOSITE

WORD PARTNERSHIP

WORD FIELD

SYNONYM OR OPPOSITE

DEFINITION

WORD FIELD

WORD FIELD

DEFINITION

SYNONYM OR OPPOSITE

WORD FIELD

DEFINITION

WORD PARTNERSHIP

WORD FIELD

DEFINITION

WORD PARTNERSHIP

SYNONYM OR OPPOSITE

WORD FIELD

WORD PARTNERSHIP

DEFINITION

SYNONYM OR OPPOSITE

WORD FIELD

SYNONYM OR OPPOSITE

WORD PARTNERSHIP

SYNONYM OR OPPOSITE

DEFINITION

WORD FIELD

DEFINITION

SYNONYM OR OPPOSITE

SYNONYM OR OPPOSITE

WORD PARTNERSHIP

WORD FIELD

DEFINITION

FINISH

VOCABULARY

grand-mother	son	step-daughter
brother-in-law	niece	twins
married	single	divorced
vegetables	fried egg	chicken
salad	pork	garlic
brown bread	salt	fruit

flat	balcony	bedroom
kitchen	coffee table	wardrobe
fridge	carpet	washbasin
train	plane	ferry
coach	bus	timetable
return ticket	under-ground	motor-bike

foggy	windy	sunny
cloudy	rainy	cool
stuffy	snow	dry
TV	music	theatre
art gallery	swimming pool	tennis court
dancing	reading	chatting

Business
English Games

The Business Grammar Game

a Business English game

In this game learners practise grammar in a business context.

Language

Level
from lower intermediate

Grammar
- adverbs of frequency: *always, never, often, sometimes, usually*
- *all, both, each other*
- comparison: *than, as ... as, not as ... as*
- future forms: *going to, will*
- *if* vs. *when*
- modal verbs: *can, could, (don't) have to, may, might, must, mustn't, should*
- passive: *is/are (done), has/have been (done), will be (done)*
- past tenses: *last week, yesterday, ago, already, ever, just, since, yet, still*
- prepositions of time: *until, by*
- Present progressive: *at the moment*
- quantifiers: *some, any, much, many, a lot, a little, a few*
- question words: *how, what, when, where, which, who*
- *so, such*

Preparation

Before the lesson
Look at the cards on pages 62–64. These contain the items in the list above and should enable learners to produce a number of useful sentences in combination with the pictures on the board (see **How to play**).

However you may prefer to use the blank cards on page 112 to give your learners a different selection or to test other items that you have been teaching recently.

You will need
- one A3-size photocopy of the board on page 61 per group of 4–6 learners;
- one cut-up set of the cards on pages 62–64 (or your own cards) per group;
- one dice per group;
- one marker per player.

The Game

Introduction
Divide learners into groups of 4–6 players. Give each group a board, dice, markers and a set of cards.

Ask learners to gather round one board. Place the cards face down on the board. Demonstrate the game by making a move and eliciting a sentence connecting one of the pictures and cards (see **Key** for examples).

The aim of the game
The winner is the first player to reach FINISH. You may wish to set a time limit rather than wait for a player to reach the final square. The winner is then the player who has made the most moves.

How to play
Players place their markers on START. The first player to throw a 6 begins. Players take it in turns to throw the dice and move around the board.

Players landing on a picture square take the top card from the pack, read it out and create a sentence that connects the two convincingly in a business context. If the rest of the group approve of the sentence, the game proceeds; if not, the player returns to his or her previous position.

Key
(some examples)

Picture: businessperson
+ Card: often

= *He/She often visits customers in ...*

Picture: plane
+ Card: ago

= *My boss flew to San Francisco two weeks ago.*

Picture: flipchart
+ Card: going to

= *I'm going to need a flipchart for my next presentation.*

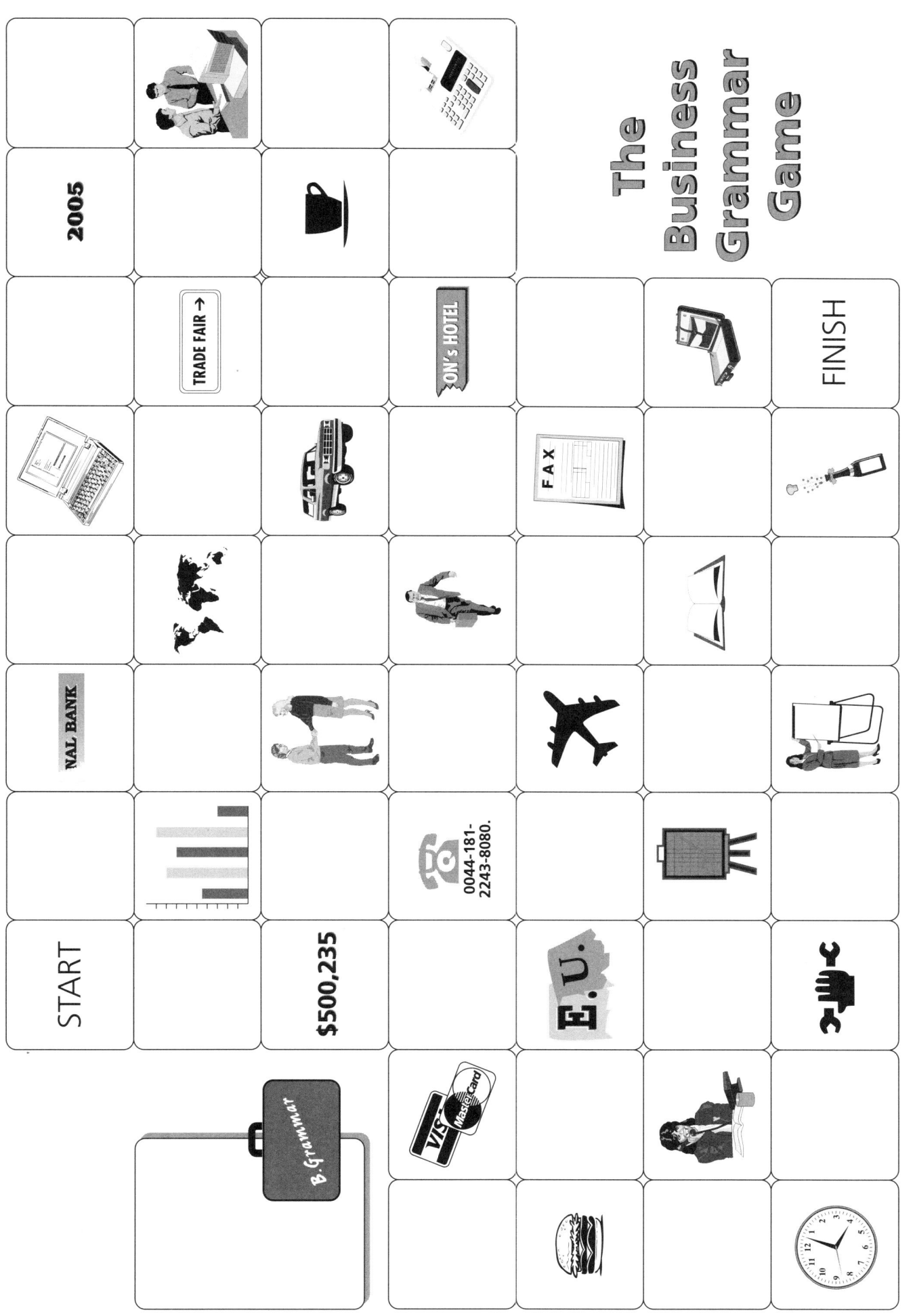

The Business Grammar Game

at the moment	sometimes	never
always	usually	often
than	as … as	not as … as
can	could	may
might	must	mustn't
have to	don't have to	should

how	what	who
when	where	which
much	many	some
any	a lot	a little
a few	so	such
all	both	each other

until	by	if
when	is/are (done)	has/have been (done)
will be (done)	last week	yesterday
ago	already	ever
just	since	yet
still	going to	will

The Business Travel Game

a Business English game

In this game learners practise language for business trips abroad.

Language

Level
from intermediate

Functions
- apologizing
- describing events
- describing the job and the working day
- describing objects
- describing towns and areas
- insisting
- making introductions
- persuading
- querying information
- regretting
- requesting help and information
- talking about change
- talking about intentions and plans
- talking about products/services
- thanking

Situations
- appointments
- car hire
- hotels
- meetings
- presentations
- restaurants

Topics
- company history
- company organization
- local customs
- travel problems
- weather

Preparation

Before the lesson
This game uses 3 sets of cards: the *Itineraries,* the *Contact* cards and the *Spot of trouble* cards. The *Itineraries* on page 69 should be used as they are. Look at the other cards on pages 70–71 and decide whether you want to use them or make your own using the blank cards on page 112.

You will need
- one A3-size photocopy of the board on page 68 per group of 4–6 learners;
- one cut-up set of the cards on pages 70–71 (or your own cards) per group;
- one cut-up set of the *Itinerary* cards on page 69 per group;
- one dice per group;
- one marker per player.

The Game

Introduction
Divide learners into groups of 4–6 players. Give each group a board, dice, markers and sets of *Contact* cards and *Spot of trouble* cards.

Ask learners to gather round one board. Place the two packs of cards face down on the board. Demonstrate the game by making one or two moves and eliciting appropriate responses (see **Key** for suggestions).

The aim of the game
The winner is the first player to arrive home, having visited and talked to the clients on his or her *Itinerary.*

How to play
Give each player an *Itinerary*. This tells them:
1. where they are at the moment;
2. where the office is that they have to return to (= home);
3. where they have to visit clients on their way home;
4. what information they have to give those clients.

Players place their markers on the city where they are at the moment. The first player to throw a 6 begins.

Players now travel to their own offices, taking in the cities specified on their *Itineraries* on the way. They can move in any direction along the route lines, but must throw the exact number to land on the cities they have to visit.

A player landing on a O or △ picks up a *Contact* or *Spot of trouble* card respectively, and responds accordingly. If the rest of the group approve of the response, the game proceeds; if not, the player returns to his or her previous position.

Key
(some possible responses)

Contact cards

Introduce yourself to some local people and say something positive about their country.
My name's … I'm from … I work for… The conference organisers have certainly chosen a beautiful city for the conference.

Comment on the weather and compare it with the climate in your home area.
Is it always so warm here at this time of year? Where I come from it's about minus ten at the moment – very cold!

Compare a custom in the country you are visiting with one in your home area.
We don't have a carnival in spring. But we have something similar in August, where people dress up and there's a procession through the streets.

Ask an Asian business partner to explain a local dish, then comment on it.
What's this called? How's it made? It's delicious!

Introduce yourself at a company reception and explain the purpose of your visit.
Good morning . My name's ... I've got an appointment to see ...

Thank your hosts for their hospitality.
Thank you very much for all your help. It's been a very pleasant trip.

Open a meeting. Greet the participants and remind them of the aim of the meeting.
Good morning everybody. Nice to see you all. I've asked you all to come today so that we can talk about ...

Give two ways of answering someone who keeps interrupting your presentation with questions.
• *Could I come back to that later?*
• *I'm glad you asked that question. I'll answer that later if you don't mind .*

You find you have spare time on a business trip. Ask a business partner about sightseeing in the area.
My flight doesn't leave until late afternoon. I'd like to look around the town. Where can I find out about a sightseeing trip – one or two hours maybe?

Talk about a new sales campaign.
You all know that we want to introduce ... into eastern Europe. Well, we plan to concentrate on TV spots on local TV stations ...

Tell a business partner about changes in your company since you last met.
Well, the sales and marketing departments have been combined ... is the new department manager – all part of our lean management programme ...

Give a brief history of your (or another) company.
• *... was founded by ... in ...*
• *We only had ... staff at the beginning.*
• *Our first ... was developed in ...*
• *Today we're world leaders in this field.*

Give a brief portrait of your town or area.
• *It's a suburb of ... with a population of 20,000.*

• *There's very little industry apart from electronics.*
• *There are several software companies in ...*

Describe your typical working day.
Well, my day usually begins at 8.30 with a briefing session. After that I check the mail and spend the rest of the day with clients or on the phone. I occasionally have lunch with a client ... and never get away before 7.00 pm.

Give a brief description of your company organization.
• *The ... group is divided into five divisions. We're in the ... division.*
• *We're a subsidiary of ...*
• *This department handles ...*
• *Fifty people work here altogether.*

Explain who you report to and what you are responsible for.
I work in human resources. My boss is ... I'm responsible for everything to do with recruitment, from adverts to the final interview.

Talk about recent trends in your industry or your country.
• *Working hours have increased rapidly this year.*
• *The textile industry has been going through a bad time.*

Close a meeting.
• *Well, thank you all – I think we've dealt with everything ...*
• *Right, so: ... will check the figures; ..., you're responsible for ... and I'll see to ...*
• *Our next meeting will be on 12 May at ...*

Spot of trouble cards

On a business trip you find that your credit card is not accepted at the hotel reception. What do you say?
• *Do you accept traveller's cheques?*
• *Is there a bank near here?*
• *Could I speak to the manager, please?*

Your flight has been cancelled and the next one is tomorrow morning. Persuade the airline staff to arrange accommodation for you.
• *What arrangements have you made for our accommodation?*
• *I'm afraid that's not acceptable.*
• *I'd like to speak to your superior, please.*
• *I'm sorry, but I'm going to stay here until you've arranged a hotel room for me.*

Describe your lost luggage to someone at the company you are visiting.
I had two suitcases, a large one and a smaller one. The large one's a ..., blue with a brown strap around it. The smaller one's a soft one made of black leather. I had them at ...

You have had an accident in a hired car. Explain what happened to the staff at the car hire office.
I had to brake suddenly because someone ran in front of the car. The driver behind me was too close and crashed into me ...

You parked your car outside the hotel. The wheels are missing. Talk to the local police.
The hotel car park was full and they told me it would be safe to park outside in the street. After breakfast I went out to the car to drive to ... and saw that all four wheels were missing ...

Your briefcase and laptop have been stolen from your car. Report the theft to the local police.
I left the car outside the bank while I was changing some money. My briefcase and laptop were on the passenger seat. When I came back one of the windows was broken and ...

You do not have some of the documents you need. Ask someone to contact your office and have them faxed to you.
Do you think you could help me, please? I have to go into the meeting now and I need some papers that I left on my desk. Could you possibly call my office and and ask Mr/Ms ... to fax them urgently? Here's the number.

Something you have eaten has disagreed with you. Explain what's wrong to someone at the company you are visiting and ask for help.
I've got terrible stomach-ache and I feel sick. I think it must be the oysters I ate yesterday evening. Do you have a doctor or someone who could give me something ...?

You have forgotten to pack socks/tights. Ask someone in the company you are visiting to help you.
I've got a small problem. I forgot to pack any ... Is there a shop nearby where I could buy some?

You are not enjoying the local food. Explain why you would like something simple to eat.
The food here is delicious, but it's a bit too rich for me and I don't usually eat meat. Do you have anything simple – like an omelette?

You have mislaid a file at the company you are visiting. Describe it to someone there.
Excuse me, but have you seen a red file with my name on it? I think I left it on Mr/Ms ...'s desk this morning ...

You seem to have arrived for a meeting on the wrong day.
- *According to my diary it's today at ... o'clock. Could I ask you to double-check?*
- *Do you think it would be possible to see Mr/Ms ... or somebody else, please? I've come all the way from ...*

The company you have to visit has two addresses in the same town. You arrive late for a meeting because you went to the wrong one.
I'm sorry I'm late, but I went to your offices on the other side of town. Your letter didn't say there are two ...

You have missed an appointment because your flight was delayed. Call the company from the airport and explain.
Hello? This is ... I'm terribly sorry I missed our appointment but my flight was delayed. We had to wait three hours before we could take off. Would it be at all possible to meet later today or tomorrow?

The American company you are visiting have invited you to their annual picnic. You do not have any informal clothes with you.
Thank you very much for the invitation, but I'm afraid I don't have the right sort of clothes with me.

You are not feeling well and want to leave a meeting. Apologize to business partners.
I'm afraid I'll have to miss the next part of the meeting and go back to my hotel. I'm not feeling very well ...

You arrive at your hotel to find that there are no rooms free. You are sure that your secretary received a fax confirming the booking.
The booking was made about two months ago and confirmed in writing. I must have a room until ...

You will be giving a presentation in a few hours. Explain what you will need and how you would like the seating arranged.
I'll need a flipchart, paper and pens and also an overhead projector. I'd like the seats arranged in a semi-circle ...

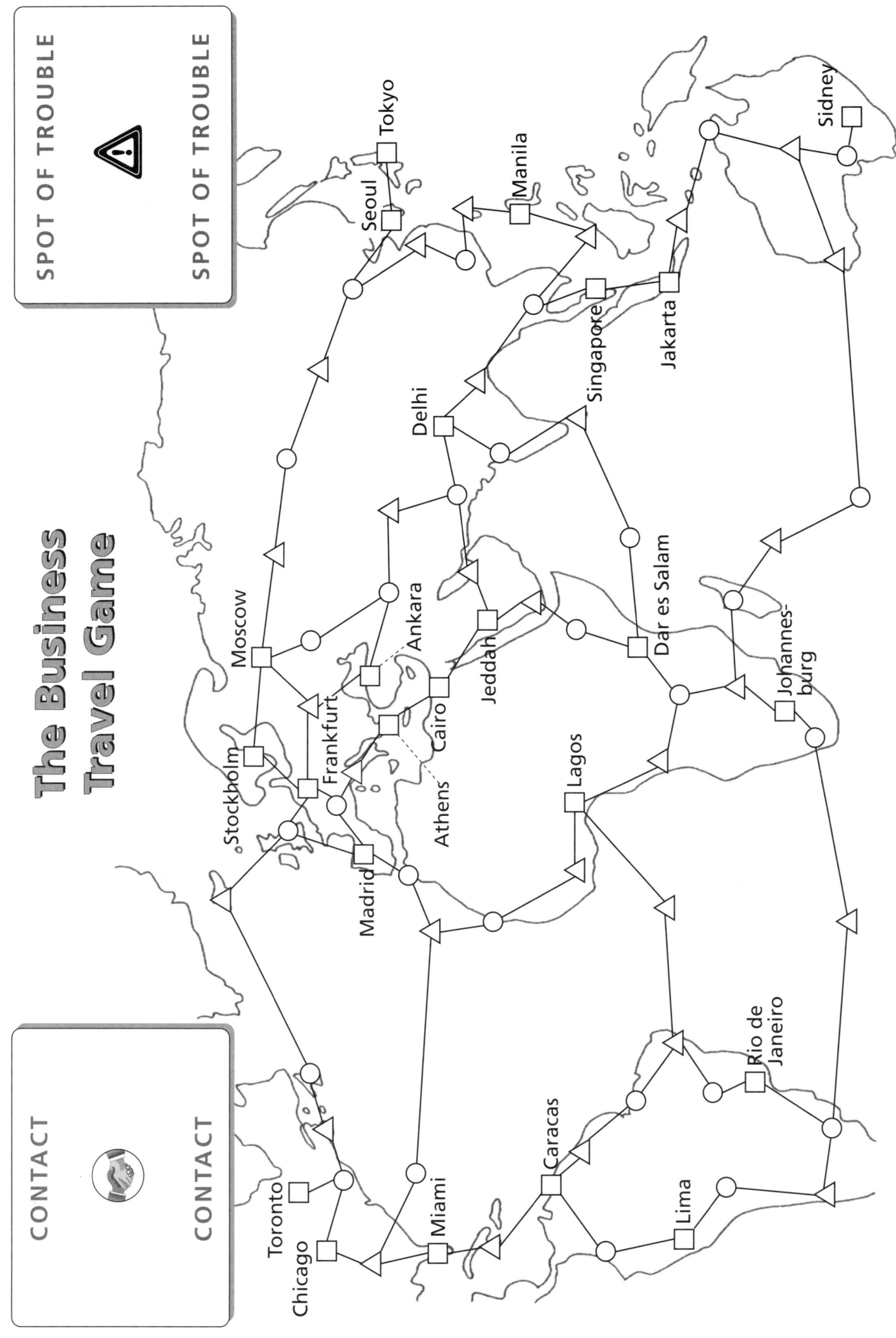

The Business Travel Game

SPOT OF TROUBLE

SPOT OF TROUBLE

CONTACT

CONTACT

Tokyo
Seoul
Manila
Sidney
Singapore
Jakarta
Delhi
Moscow
Ankara
Jeddah
Dar es Salam
Johannesburg
Stockholm
Frankfurt
Cairo
Athens
Lagos
Madrid
Caracas
Rio de Janeiro
Lima
Toronto
Chicago
Miami

Itinerary 3

At the moment you are in Chicago, but your office is in Dar es Salaam. Visit clients in Jeddah and Moscow on your way home.
Choose two of these topics to talk about with your clients:

- A new product or service.
- Why one of your products or services is successful
- A new product or service compared with its predecessor.
- One of your products or services compared with the competition.
  - Your main markets.
  - Changes in the market.

Itinerary 6

At the moment you are in Rio de Janeiro, but your office is in Singapore. Visit clients in Ankara and Madrid on your way home.
Choose two of these topics to talk about with your clients:

- A new product or service.
- Why one of your products or services is successful
- A new product or service compared with its predecessor.
- One of your products or services compared with the competition.
  - Your main markets.
  - Changes in the market.

Itinerary 2

At the moment you are in Cairo, but your office is in Toronto. Visit clients in Caracas and Lagos on your way home.
Choose two of these topics to talk about with your clients:

- A new product or service.
- Why one of your products or services is successful.
- A new product or service compared with its predecessor.
- One of your products or services compared with the competition.
  - Your main markets.
  - Changes in the market.

Itinerary 5

At the moment you are in Tokyo, but your office is in Lima. Visit clients in Miami and Stockholm on your way home.
Choose two of these topics to talk about with your clients:

- A new product or service.
- Why one of your products or services is successful.
- A new product or service compared with its predecessor.
- One of your products or services compared with the competition.
  - Your main markets.
  - Changes in the market.

Itinerary 1

At the moment you are in Sydney, but your office is in Frankfurt. Visit clients in Athens and Delhi on your way home.
Choose two of these topics to talk about with your clients:

- A new product or service.
- Why one of your products or services is successful.
- A new product or service compared with its predecessor.
- One of your products or services compared with the competition.
  - Your main markets.
  - Changes in the market.

Itinerary 4

At the moment you are in Johannesburg, but your office is in Seoul. Visit clients in Manila and Jakarta on your way home.
Choose two of these topics to talk about with your clients:

- A new product or service.
- Why one of your products or services is successful.
- A new product or service compared with its predecessor.
- One of your products or services compared with the competition.
  - Your main markets.
  - Changes in the market.

Introduce yourself to some local people and say something positive about their country.

Comment on the weather and compare it with the climate in your home area.

Compare a custom in the country you are visiting with one in your home area.

Ask an Asian business partner to explain a local dish, then comment on it.

Introduce yourself at a company reception and explain the purpose of your visit.

Thank your hosts for their hospitality.

Open a meeting. Greet the participants and remind them of the aim of the meeting.

Give two ways of answering someone who keeps interrupting your presentation with questions.

You find you have spare time on a business trip. Ask a business partner about sightseeing in the area.

Talk about a new sales campaign.

Tell a business partner about changes in your company since you last met.

Give a brief history of your (or another) company.

Give a brief portrait of your town or area.

Describe your typical working day.

Give a brief description of your company organization.

Explain who you report to and what you are responsible for.

Talk about recent trends in your industry or your country.

Close a meeting.

On a business trip you find that your credit card is not accepted at the hotel reception. What do you say?

Your flight has been cancelled and the next one is tomorrow morning. Persuade the airline staff to arrange accommodation for you.

Describe your lost luggage to someone at the company you are visiting.

You have had an accident in a hired car. Explain what happened to the staff at the car hire office.

You parked your car outside the hotel. The wheels are missing. Talk to the local police.

Your briefcase and laptop have been stolen from your car. Report the theft to the local police.

You do not have some of the documents you need. Ask someone to contact your office and have them faxed to you.

Something you have eaten has disagreed with you. Explain what's wrong to someone at the company you are visiting and ask for help.

You have forgotten to pack socks/tights. Ask someone in the company you are visiting to help you.

You are not enjoying the local food. Explain why you would like something simple to eat.

You have mislaid a file at the company you are visiting. Describe it to someone there.

You seem to have arrived for a meeting on the wrong day.

The company you have to visit has two addresses in the same town. You arrive late for a meeting because you went to the wrong one.

You have missed an appointment because your flight was delayed. Call the company from the airport and explain.

The American company you are visiting have invited you to their annual picnic. You do not have any informal clothes with you.

You are not feeling well and want to leave a meeting. Apologize to business partners.

You arrive at your hotel to find that there are no rooms free. You are sure that your secretary received a fax confirming the booking.

You will be giving a presentation in a few hours. Explain what you will need and how you would like the seating arranged.

The Business Vocabulary Game

a Business English game

In this game learners practise their business vocabulary.

Language

Level
any level

Vocabulary
Any vocabulary that you want your learners to revise.

Preparation

Before the lesson
Look at the cards on pages 74–76. These contain some useful vocabulary from the fields of *company organization and premises, departments, daily work, occupations, appointments and sales*, and are given to show how the game is played. You will probably want to make your own selection of vocabulary that your learners have been working on recently, using the blank cards on page 112.

You will need
- one A3-size photocopy of the board on page 73 per group of 4 learners;
- one cut-up set of the cards on pages 74–76 (or your own cards) per group;
- one dice per group;
- one marker per player.

The Game

Introduction
Divide learners into groups of 4 players. Give each group a board, dice, markers and a set of cards.

Ask learners to gather round one board. Place the cards face down on the board. Demonstrate the game by making one or two moves and eliciting appropriate responses.

The aim of the game
The winner is the first player to reach FINISH. You may wish to set a time limit rather than wait for a player to reach the final square. The winner is then the player who has made the most moves.

How to play
Players (or teams) place their markers on START. The first player to throw a 6 begins. Players take it in turns to throw the dice and move around the board.

Players landing on a square take the top card from the pack and respond according to the instruction on the square. If the rest of the group approve of the response, the game proceeds; if not, the player returns to his or her previous position.

Key
(some examples)

Definition
Learner gives a definition of the word on the card, e.g. *This word means ....*

Synonym or Opposite
Learner thinks of a synonym or opposite for the word on the card, e.g. *invoice – bill* or *parent company – subsidiary.*

(N.B. It may not always be possible to find a synonym or opposite, in which case learners have to pass.)

Word field
Learners think of at least two other words in the same word field as the word on the card, e.g. *discount – full price – offer.*

Word partnership
Learner thinks of a partnership for the word on the card, e.g. *arrange – arrange a meeting.*

"Looking at Holligan it's hard to believe he possesses strong leadership and supervisory skills, is self-motivated, has a proven track record, is enterprising, energetic, creative, degreed and seeks a challenge."

The Business Vocabulary Game

START

FINISH

VOCABULARY

DEFINITION → WORD-FIELD

WORD PARTNER-SHIP → WORD-FIELD

WORD PARTNER-SHIP

WORD PARTNER-SHIP

SYNONYM OR OPPOSITE

SYNONYM OR OPPOSITE

SYNONYM OR OPPOSITE

SYNONYM OR OPPOSITE

DEFINITION

WORD PARTNER-SHIP

WORD-FIELD → WORD PARTNER-SHIP

WORD-FIELD

DEFINITION

WORD-FIELD

DEFINITION

SYNONYM OR OPPOSITE

SYNONYM OR OPPOSITE

DEFINITION

WORD PARTNER-SHIP

SYNONYM OR OPPOSITE

WORD-FIELD

WORD PARTNER-SHIP

DEFINITION

WORD PARTNER-SHIP

WORD-FIELD

DEFINITION

WORD PARTNER-SHIP

DEFINITION

WORD-FIELD

SYNONYM OR OPPOSITE → WORD PARTNER-SHIP

SYNONYM OR OPPOSITE

WORD-FIELD

WORD PARTNER-SHIP

DEFINITION

SYNONYM OR OPPOSITE

SYNONYM OR OPPOSITE

WORD-FIELD → DEFINITION

parent company	headquarters	subsidiary
branch	department	office
canteen	car park	elevator
personnel	EDP (electronic data processing)	accounts
production	R & D (research and development)	maintenance
market research	advertising	sales

clock in	flexitime	lunch break
overtime	office hours	deadline
meeting	phone call	correspondence
porter	secretary	salesperson
accountant	lawyer	security guard
technician	designer	trainee

The Business Vocabulary Game · Cards

arrange	convenient	abroad
diary	busy	schedule
date	postpone	bring forward
target	figures	customer
brochure	retail price	order
invoice	discount	delivery

The Business Vocabulary Game · Cards

The Facts & Figures Game

a Business English game

In this game learners practise giving information, with the emphasis on various kinds of numbers.

Language

Level
from lower intermediate

Topics / Functions / Vocabulary
- alphabet
- arithmetic
- cardinal and ordinal numbers
- checking and clarifying information
- date
- decimals
- fractions
- giving and requesting information
- price
- telephone numbers
- temperature
- time
- weights and measures

Preparation

Before the lesson
Decide whether you want to use the cards on page 80 or make your own using the blank cards on page 112.

You will need
- one A3-size photocopy of the board on page 79 per group of 4–6 learners;
- one cut-up set of the cards on page 80 (or your own cards) per group;
- one dice per group;
- one marker per player.

The Game

Introduction
Divide learners into groups of 4–6 players. Give each group a board, dice, markers and a set of cards.

Ask learners to gather round one board. Place the cards face down on the board. Demonstrate the game by making one or two moves and eliciting appropriate responses (see **Key** for suggestions).

The aim of the game
The winner is the first player to reach FINISH. You may wish to set a time limit rather than wait for a player to reach the final square. The winner is then the player who has made the most moves.

How to play
Players place their markers on START. The first player to throw a 6 begins. Players take it in turns to throw the dice and move around the board.

A player landing on a square with a task reads it out and responds accordingly, interacting with a partner if necessary.

Players landing on a square with an F&F symbol take the top card from the pack, read it out and carry out the task. If the rest of the group approve of the response, the game proceeds; if not, the player returns to his or her previous position.

Key
(some possible responses)

1. A reporter asks for some information about your company.
   Our company produces ... ; we have a subsidiary in ... and employ 1,200 people.

2. Say what the dollar rate is at the moment.
   - *There are about ... to the ... at the moment.*
   - *It's about ... today.*

4. Spell your name and address on an answer phone.
   My name's Ann Schmid. That's A-N-N, new word S-C-H-M-I-D. My address is ...

5. Say these numbers: 2,000,000,000; 321,897; 91,624
   - *two billion;*
   - *three hundred (and) twenty-one thousand, eight hundred (and) ninety-seven;*
   - *ninety-one thousand, six hundred (and) twenty-four.*

6. What's the population of your town?
   About 150,000.

7. Give someone a brief version of your CV.
   - *I started work in ...*
   - *My first job was at/with ...*
   - *I stayed there for ... years.*
   - *In ... I moved/was transferred/promoted to ...*

9. Tell a visitor about summer and winter temperatures in your region.
   In winter it's usually very cold, from minus 1 to minus 10 degrees, and in summer it can be from 18 to 37 degrees.

10. Describe an important trade fair in your area.
    The Boat Show takes place every autumn. You can see the latest boats – speed boats, yachts ...

11. Give someone details of a bank account.
I have an account with ... Bank. My account number is ... and the bank code is ...

13. Tell a visitor about a local company.
... is the largest factory in our area. They produce ladies' clothes and export them all over the world.

14. Give details of a delivery date.
We can deliver next week, on Monday or Tuesday – that's the 17th or 18th of March.

16. Say these numbers: $5^{3}/_{4}$; $6^{7}/_{8}$; $10^{2}/_{3}$
   - *five and three-quarters;*
   - *six and seven-eighths;*
   - *ten and two-thirds.*

17. Talk about working hours in your company.
We work from ... to ..., with a half an hour break for lunch.

18. Ask for details of a product.
   - *Could you give me some information about ...?*
   - *How big is ...?*

20. Give a visitor information on the type of industry in your area.
In our area there are many electronics companies, for example ...

21. Give details of a product range.
We have a wide range of software – for word processing, home banking, tax problems ... we also have CAD (computer-assisted design) programs.

23. Give a customer some information about a product.
This is our new model. It's about 20 cm long and weighs 2 kilos. It's very easy to operate.

24. Say these prices: ¥581,267,000; $29,012.00
   - *five hundred (and) eighty-one million, two hundred (and) sixty-seven thousand yen;*
   - *twenty-nine thousand and twelve dollars.*

25. Talk about food prices in your country.
Food is very expensive today. Meat costs ..., bread costs ... per kilo and coffee costs ... per pound.

26. What can you say if you want to check information?
   - *Did you say "Paris" or "Paros"?*
   - *Could you tell me exactly what ...?*

28. Say these numbers: 3.55%; 5.96%; 0.78%
   - *three point five five per cent;*
   - *five point nine six per cent;*
   - *nought/zero point seven eight per cent.*

29. Compare two products you know.
The ... model is much larger than ... and costs twice as much.

31. Call a foreign colleague and give him/her the date and time of a meeting.
Our next sales conference is on 28th October, starting at nine thirty.

32. Say this calculation: 15 + 40 - 5 = 50
Fifteen plus/and forty minus/less five equals/is fifty.

33. Say the following: 32 m^2; 109 cm^3.
   - *thirty-two square metres;*
   - *one hundred (and) nine cubic centimetres.*

35. Say the telephone numbers of two people or organizations.
oh/zero eight nine – five three six two one seven: that's my sister's number; ...

36. Say these numbers: 9 mm; 10 cm; 4.8 m.
   - *nine millimetres;*
   - *ten centimetres;*
   - *four point eight metres.*

37. What can you say if you don't have the facts a business partner needs?
   - *I'm sorry, I don't know. I'll find out.*
   - *I'm afraid I haven't got the information at the moment, but I'll get back to you as soon as I can.*

39. Compare the cost of public and private transport.
Well, travelling by train isn't cheap, but if you add up what a car really costs to run ...

40. Say this calculation: 113 x 30 ÷ 2 = 1695.
one hundred (and) thirteen times/multiplied by thirty divided by two equals/is one thousand six hundred (and) ninety-five

THE FACTS & FIGURES GAME

START

A reporter asks for some information about your company.	Say these numbers: 3.55%; 5.96%; 0.78%.
Say what the dollar rate is at the moment.	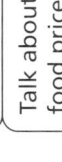
F&F	What can you say if you want to check information?
Spell your name and address on an answer phone.	Talk about food prices in your country.
Call a foreign colleague and give him/her the date and time of a meeting.	Say these prices: ¥581,267,00; $29,012,00.
Say this calculation: 15+40-5=50	Give a customer some information about a Product.

F&F

FINISH

Say the following: 32m²; 109cm³.	Say this calculation: 113x30÷2=1695.
Give someone a brief version of your CV.	Give details of a product range.
What's the population of your town?	Give a visitor information on the type of industry in your area.
Say these numbers: 2,000,000; 321,897; 91,624.	Ask for details of a product.

GAME

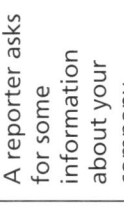

Tell a visitor about summer and winter temperatures in your region.	Talk about working hours in your company.
Describe an important trade fair in your area.	
Say the telephone numbers of two people or organizations.	Say these numbers: 5 ³/₄; 6 ⁷/₈; 10 ²/₃.
Say these numbers: 9 mm; 10 cm; 4.8 m.	
What can you say if you don't have the facts a business partner needs?	

Give someone details of a bank account.

Tell a visitor about a local company.

Give details of a delivery date.

F&F

<table>
<tr><td>

Compare with your country.

Tipping in the UK

Restaurants	10-15%
Cafés	Leave small change
Taxis	10%

</td><td>

Tell the other players about these investments.

Franchising opportunities

Name	Nature	No.of outlets	Min. investmt.
Stars	Toy shops	20	$ 55,000
Milki	Milk bars	400	$120,000
Catto	Pet shops	50	$ 78,000

</td><td>

Tell the other players about your itinerary.

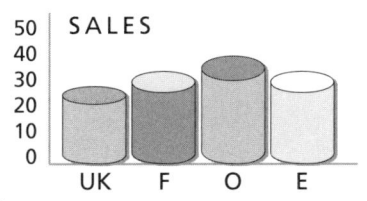

Mon. 10
- Paris: 10.00–16.00 Europ. Sales Mgrs Conf. 19.00 Dinner
Tues. 11
- Brussels: 13.30 Presentation
Wed. 12
- Brussels: (time?) Visit LNP

</td></tr>

<tr><td>

Give the other players some information about this person.

"Business of the Year"
Winner: John Lewis
Company: US Medcars
Business: Ambulance service
Founded: 1992
Revenues: $327m
Profits: $27m
No.of employees: 6,200

</td><td>

BUSINESS ORGANIZER

Desk model A4 size
with 6-ring mechanism

Leather (black or burgundy)
complete with fill $64.55

</td><td>

Explain this bar chart to the other players.

SALES

</td></tr>

<tr><td>

Explain this pie chart to the other players.

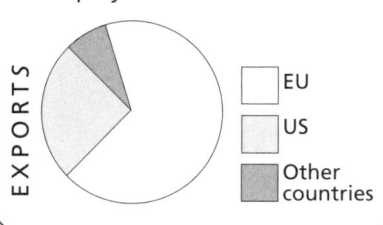

EXPORTS

- EU
- US
- Other countries

</td><td>

Explain this graph to the other players.

PRODUCTION

</td><td>

Explain this section of an organigram to the other players.

CEO
Sales & Mktg Director
Sales Mgr — Mktg Mgr
Southern region Sales Coord. — Northern region Sales Coord.

</td></tr>

<tr><td>

Describe this advertisement to the other players.

GLOBAL TELEPHONE
Easy-to-use satellite telephone
- Made in Germany
- Unbeatable price
- Available now!

SAT TEC   SAT TEC

</td><td>

Tell the other players how to get your office (X) from the station.

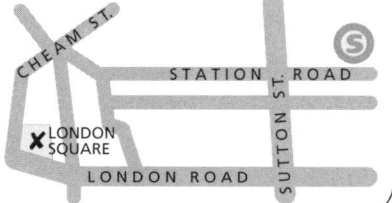

CHEAM ST.   STATION ST. ROAD   SUTTON ST. ROAD
X LONDON SQUARE
LONDON ROAD

</td><td>

A Danish friend is looking for a job. Tell the other players about him.

English-speaking Dane, 29
Personnel management experience. Excellent organizer.
Fluent German. Good English.
Seeking position in UK/USA.

</td></tr>

<tr><td>

Tell the other players about the weather in 3 cities.

Weekend weather	min	max	sky
Amsterdam	2	9	RS
Athens	10	15	PC
Brussels	3	9	RS
Copenhagen	4	4	PB

</td><td>

What interests men?

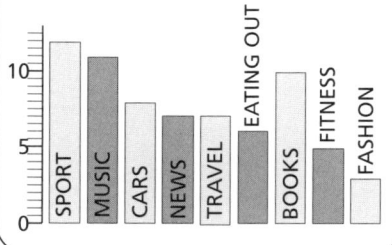

SPORT, MUSIC, CARS, NEWS, TRAVEL, BOOKS, EATING OUT, FITNESS, FASHION

</td><td>

Tell the other players about hotel prices.

Single room	$175
Double room	$210

Weekend rates (2 nights)
Single room	$220
Double room	$250

* All rates include buffet-breakfast, service charge and VAT.

</td></tr>

<tr><td>

Tell the other players about the cost of this paper in 4 countries.

The Daily Continental: European prices

Austria	S	35
Belgium	BF	65
Czech Rep.	KC	75
Denmark	KR	18.00
Finland	MK	16.00
France	FF	18.00
German	DM	5.00

</td><td>

Tell your boss about the hotel you have booked for a sales conference.

Bridge Hall
Near Manchester
Quiet conference centre in 18th C. house set in beautiful park. Four-star accommodation and cuisine. Caters for 2-350. Choice of meeting rooms. Tennis, golf, fishing facilities.
For information please contact Jenny Wisdon on +49 (0)161 232 664820

</td><td>

Tell the other players about this job ad.

PRODUCT DEVELOPMENT MANAGER
required for French designer shoe sales. Expertise in planning budgets, marketing campaigns in the UK and developing markets in China and SE Asia. Ability to communicate in French and Mandarin essential. Salary negotiable.

</td></tr>
</table>

The Intercultural Game

a Business English game

In this game learners talk about cultural differences, including values and attitudes, body language and local customs. They also try to explain some intercultural misunderstandings.

Language

Level
from intermediate

Topics
- describing cultural misunderstandings
- describing customs and events
- talking about life and work in other cultures
- talking about your own culture

Preparation

Before the lesson
This game uses 4 different packs of cards: *At work, Customs & events, Other cultures* and *Intercultural clashes*. Each pack contains 9 cards. Look at the cards on pages 85–86 and decide whether you want to use them or make your own using the blank cards on page 112.

You will need
- one A3-size photocopy of the board on page 84 per group of 4 learners;
- one cut-up set of the cards on pages 85–86 (or your own cards) per group;
- one dice per group;
- one marker per player.

The Game

Introduction
Divide learners into groups of 4 (one player for each corner of the board). Give each group a board, dice, markers and a full set of 36 cards.

Ask learners to gather round one board. Place the 4 packs of cards face down on the board. Demonstrate the game by making one or two moves and eliciting suitable responses (see **Key** for suggestions).

The aim of the game
The winner is the first player to reach FINISH. You may wish to set a time limit rather than wait for a player to reach the middle of the board. The winner is then the player who has made the most moves.

How to play
Each player chooses a corner of the board and places his or her marker on START. The first player to throw a 6 begins. Players take it in turns to throw the dice and move around their corner of the board.

Players landing on a square take the top card from the appropriate pack, read it out and respond accordingly, interacting with a partner if necessary. If the rest of the group approve of the response, the game proceeds; if not, the player returns to his or her previous position.

You will probably need to approve learners' solutions to the *Intercultural clashes* (see Card set 4) – suggested answers for these are given in the **Key**.

Key
(some possible responses)

Card set 1: *At work*

Is it acceptable to receive gifts from business partners in your country?
Small gifts at Christmas-time are alright, but you should be careful if a supplier offers you more than that.

Talk about office hours in your country.
- *In most firms you have to start by 8.30.*
- *In companies with flexitime systems you can usually leave around 3.30.*

Talk about titles and first names at work in your country.
- *Titles are very important in our country.*
- *People with doctorates or professorships expect their titles to be used.*
- *No one uses first names in the office.*

How do business people dress in your country?
- *We have to/don't have to wear ...*
- *Most people wear ...*

How important is punctuality at work in your country?
We expect people to be punctual for business appointments.

What part does humour play at work in your country?
People make jokes among themselves, of course, but not in a board meeting or when they're dealing with customers.

How do you entertain business partners in your country?
We usually take them to a good restaurant.

Talk about women in management in your country.
It's still fairly unusual for a senior manager to be a woman.

How often do colleagues socialize outside working hours in your country?
Not very often. Most people try to keep their private life separate from their work.

Card set 2: *Customs & events*

Talk about a local or national religious custom.
We celebrate the sixth of January, that's Epiphany, and we give each other presents ...

Talk about a public holiday in your country.
We have a holiday on ... That's our national day. We ...

Describe a spring or summer custom in your country.
We have parties, balls and dress up in ...
We celebrate the end of winter ...

Talk about an autumn or winter custom in your country.
We decorate front doors with a wreath made of twigs and berries ...

What sort of music or musical instruments are typical of your area?
There's a special instrument we play for dancing. It's a sort of ...

Describe any traditional clothes from your country or region.
Some of the older people still wear baggy black trousers and headbands.

Talk about a famous local man or woman.
The most famous person from our area was a writer called ...

Describe a local speciality.
We have a regional dish called ... It's made of ...

Talk about a custom that foreigners think is typical of your country.
They seem to think we all walk around dressed up in ... and eat ... every day.

Card set 3: *Other cultures*

Talk about table manners in another country.
When I was in the States, people cut up all their food first and then ate it with their forks.

Talk about drinks in another country.
In the Middle East they drink a lot of peppermint tea. It's very refreshing ...

Talk about working in another country.
They say that the Japanese work much harder than we do, and that they have to go out drinking with colleagues after work. I wouldn't want to do that.

Talk about clothes in another country.
In the city of London some men still wear bowler hats.

Talk about gestures in another country.
Be careful giving a "V for Victory" sign in Britain. If you get it the wrong way round, it is a serious insult.

Talk about a country you would like to live in for a year.
I'd love to live in Crete for a while; the people are really friendly and the landscape is amazing ...

Talk about body language in another country.
In the warmer countries, people seem to stand closer together and touch each other more when they are speaking.

Talk about shopping in another country.
- *In London you can do your food shopping at 10 p.m. if you want to – and buy your clothes in a big store on a Sunday.*
- *I find I don't like shopping in countries where they expect you to bargain. It just doesn't come naturally to me ...*

Talk about a festival in another country.
On November 5th the British celebrate Guy Fawkes' Night with big bonfires and fireworks. Guy Fawkes tried to blow up the Houses of Parliament ...

Card set 4: *Intercultural clashes*

A British couple were surprised when the German business partner they had invited to dinner handed them a bunch of flowers. Why?
The visitor unwrapped the flowers before handing them to his hosts. In Britain this is a bit like saying "Look at these beautiful flowers I've brought you!"

The American businessman was worried about his Thai partners. They seemed very competent, but somehow he just didn't trust them. Why not?
Like a number of other nationalities, Thais consider it impolite to deal eye-to-eye, whereas Americans and Europeans tend to be suspicious of someone who refuses to meet their gaze.

British visitors to Germany sometimes find it difficult to walk along busy pedestrian streets. Why?
Unlike the British, Germans normally walk on the right.

Another passenger looked irritated when a foreigner opened a train window on a hot day in England. Why?
The visitor simply opened the window. In Britain it is normal to ask "Do you mind if I open the window?" before doing so.

A Japanese businessman gave his card to a European sitting next to him, who took it and put it in his pocket. Why was the Japanese offended?
Japanese protocol requires that business cards are exchanged, held in both hands and looked at respectfully.

A foreign visitor had to go to the doctor in Britain. When he walked into the waiting-room and said "Good morning," the other patients looked uncomfortable. Why?
British people do not normally greet strangers in public places such as waiting rooms, lifts and trains.

Some British visitors were surprised when the main course in a German canteen was a sweet dish.
People in Anglo-Saxon countries normally only eat sweet dishes for dessert.

A young Swiss engineer enjoyed his visit to the pub with the English members of his project team, but he wasn't invited again. Why not?
By the time he had realized that he was expected to buy a round of drinks for the rest of the group, the evening was over.

You went into a restaurant in Britain and sat down, but the waiter asked you to move. Why?
In Britain, as in America, your normally have to wait for the waiter to find you somewhere to sit.

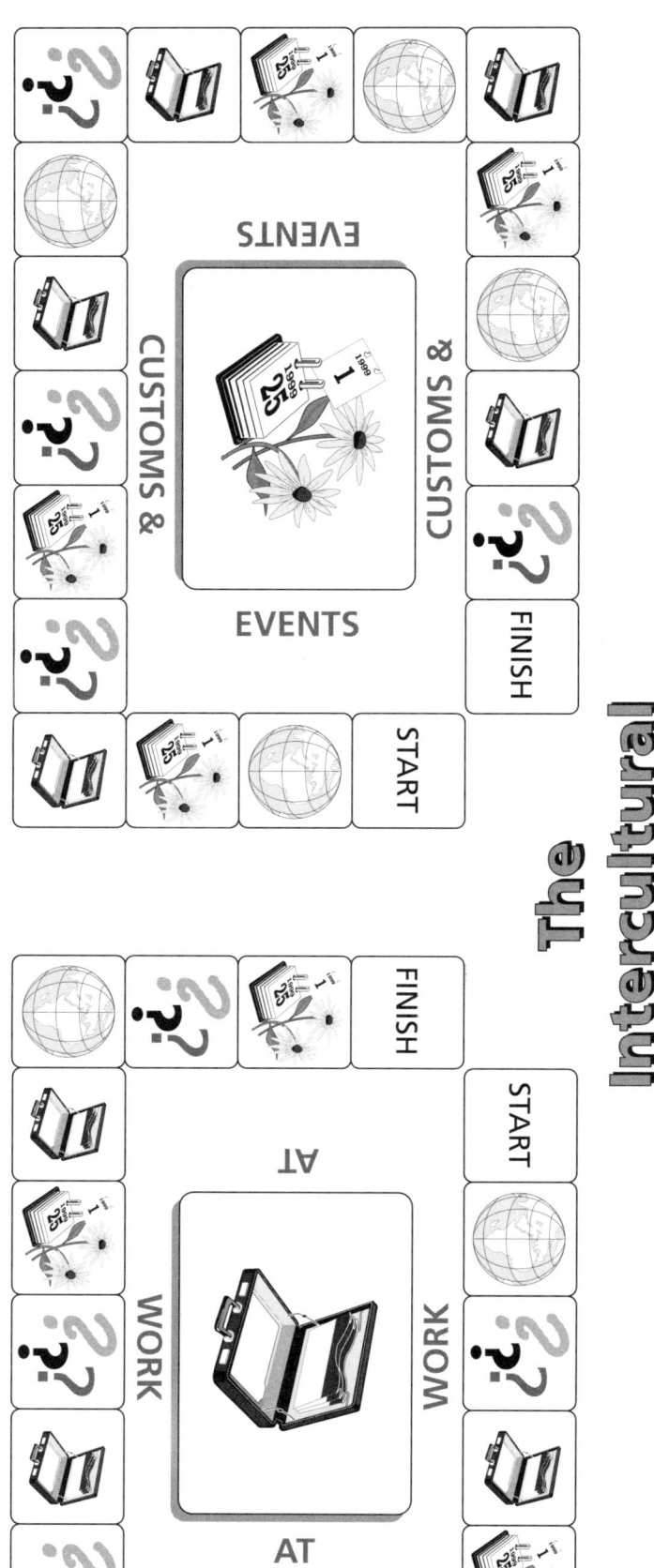

CUSTOMS & EVENTS

CUSTOMS & EVENTS

EVENTS

START

FINISH

INTERCULTURAL CLASHES

CLASHES

INTERCULTURAL

INTERCULTURAL CLASHES

START

FINISH

The Intercultural Game

AT WORK

AT WORK

WORK

AT

START

FINISH

OTHER CULTURES

OTHER

CULTURES

CULTURES

OTHER

START

FINISH

Is it acceptable to receive gifts from business partners in your country?

Talk about office hours in your country.

Talk about titles and first names at work in your country.

How do business people dress in your country?

How important is punctuality at work in your country?

What part does humour play at work in your country?

How do you entertain business partners in your country?

Talk about women in management in your country.

How often do colleagues socialize outside working hours in your country?

Talk about a local or national religious custom.

Talk about a public holiday in your country.

Describe a spring or summer custom in your country.

Talk about an autumn or winter custom in your country.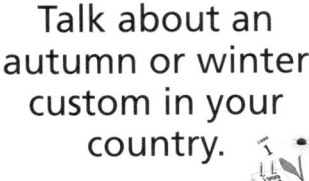

What sort of music or musical instruments are typical of your area?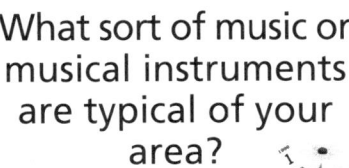

Describe any traditional clothes from your country or region.

Talk about a famous local man or woman.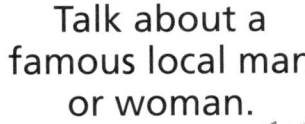

Describe a local speciality.

Talk about a custom that foreigners think is typical of your country.

Talk about table manners in another country.

Talk about drinks in another country.

Talk about working in another country.

Talk about clothes in another country.

Talk about gestures in another country.

Talk about a country you would like to live in for a year.

Talk about body language in another country.

Talk about shopping in another country.

Talk about a festival in another country.

A British couple were surprised when the German business partner they had invited to dinner handed them a bunch of flowers. Why?

The American businessman was worried about his Thai partners. They seemed very competent, but somehow he just didn't trust them. Why not?

British visitors to Germany sometimes find it difficult to walk along busy pedestrian streets. Why?

Another passenger looked irritated when a foreigner opened a train window on a hot day in England. Why?

A Japanese businessman gave his card to a European sitting next to him, who took it and put it in his pocket. Why was the Japanese offended?

A foreign visitor had to go to the doctor in Britain. When he walked into the waiting-room and said "Good morning," the other patients looked un-comfortable. Why?

Some English visitors were surprised when the main course in a German canteen was a sweet dish.

A young Swiss engineer enjoyed his visit to the pub with the English members of his project team, but he wasn't invited again. Why not?

You went into a restaurant in Britain and sat down, but the waiter asked you to move. Why?

The Management Game

a Business English game

In this game learners talk about presentations, negotiations, meetings and problem situations.

Language

Level
from intermediate

Presentations
- introducing and thanking presenters
- equipment
- diagrams
- asking for elaboration
- dealing with questions

Negotiations
- negotiations vocabulary
- terms and conditions
- persuading
- bargaining

Meetings
- meetings vocabulary
- opening and closing meetings
- interrupting
- disagreeing

Hazards
dealing with tricky situations

Preparation

Before the lesson
This game uses 4 different packs of cards: *Presentations*, *Negotiations*, *Meetings* and *Hazards*. Each pack contains 9 cards. Look at the cards on pages 91–92 and decide whether you want to use them or make your own using the blank cards on page 112.

You will need
- one A3-size photocopy of the board on page 90 per group of 4 learners;
- one cut-up set of the cards on pages 91–92 (or your own cards) per group;
- one dice per group;
- one marker per player.

The Game

Introduction
Divide learners into groups of 4 (one player for each corner of the board). Give each group a board, dice, markers and a full set of 36 cards.

Ask learners to gather round one board. Place the 4 packs of cards face down on the board. Demonstrate the game by making one or two moves and eliciting appropriate responses (see **Key** for suggestions).

The aim of the game
The winner is the first player to reach FINISH. You may wish to set a time limit rather than wait for a player to reach the middle of the board. The winner is then the player who has made the most moves.

How to play
Each player chooses a corner of the board and places his or her marker on START. The first player to throw a 6 begins. Players take it in turns to throw the dice and move around their corner of the board.

Players landing on a square take the top card from the appropriate pack, read it out and respond accordingly, interacting with a partner if necessary. If the rest of the group approve of the response, the game proceeds; if not, the player returns to his or her previous position.

Key
(some possible responses)

Card set 1: *Presentations*

Introduce the guest speaker at an international conference.
Ladies and gentlemen, it gives me great pleasure to introduce ... who is going to speak to us about ...

Talk about equipment for presentations.
Well, when I have to make a presentation I normally ask for an OHP (overhead projector) and a flip-chart. I sometimes use a video or slide projector too.

Give your opinion on what makes a good presentation.
A clear structure, good visuals, clear speech ...

Describe two mistakes that presenters sometimes make.
- *Reading their presentation instead of speaking freely.*
- *Speaking to their visuals instead of to the audience.*
- *Addressing their presentation to the most important person in the room.*

When might you use these expressions in a presentation?
Now let's look at ... / As you can see ...
To focus the attention of the audience on a visual of some kind.

You are attending a presentation. Ask for more information about a particular point.
- *Could I go back to what you said about ...?*
- *You mentioned ...; could you tell us ...?*

Someone tries to catch you out with a difficult question during a presentation.
- *That's a very interesting question. What would you say?*
- *I'll get back to you on that one.*
- *Perhaps we could discuss that later.*

At the end of a presentation, someone asks a question you can't answer.
- *That's a good question; I wish I knew the answer!*
- *I'm afraid we haven't got an answer to that one yet. But we're working on it.*

Thank a presenter.
On behalf of everyone here, I'd like to thank Mr/Ms ... for a most informative talk ...

Card set 2: *Negotiations*

Comment on this statement:
"It's better to be the buyer than the seller in a negotiation."
(personalized comment)

Complete this sentence: "Good negotiators ..."
- *... prepare a number of options.*
- *... don't give away their strategy.*

Think of at least four words in the "negotiate" word family.
negotiator, negotiation, negotiable, non-negotiable, negotiability

Think of at least three verbs that can be used with the word "contract" (e.g. to negotiate a contract).
to draw up a contract, to sign a contract, to renew a contract, to cancel a contract

What needs to be considered before negotiating a sales contract?
Price; delivery time and transport; terms of payment; insurance ...

The price you have been quoted for some new office equipment is far too high. Negotiate a reduction.
- *Is that your best offer?*
- *What sort of discount do you offer for prompt payment?*
- *We're very interested in your products, but I'm afraid we're going to have to look again at other suppliers.*

Your company hires out executive jets. Explain your terms to a potential customer, using two of these expressions: as a rule / on condition that / even if / unless.
- *As a rule we don't hire out aircraft for less than a week; however ...*

- *Customers are allowed to use their own pilots on condition that they have a current licence and have logged at least ... flying hours in the last ...*
- *The full hire charge must be paid even if bad weather makes it impossible to fly.*
- *Customers are liable for any damage to the plane unless this is due to mechanical failure ...*

Your boss has asked you to sort out a problem in a difficult country. This will take at least nine months. What terms would you negotiate?
- *I would insist on my current job being kept open for me.*
- *The firm would have to provide and pay for my accommodation in the other country.*
- *He would have to agree to fly me home once a month for a few days at the firm's expense.*

Your assistant may resign unless he or she is given a substantial rise. This would be difficult at present. Negotiate a solution.
- *As I'm sure you know, the current financial situation ...*
- *I can promise you that as soon as things begin to look up ...*
- *What I could offer you right away would be ...*

Card set 3: *Meetings*

Think of at least three verbs that can be used with the word "meeting" (e.g. to organize a meeting).
to hold a meeting, to attend a meeting, to chair a meeting, to postpone a meeting, to cancel a meeting

One of your colleagues has to chair an important meeting for the first time. Give him or her three tips.
- *Welcome the participants at the beginning and thank them at the end.*
- *Arrange for someone to take the minutes.*
- *Make sure everyone has a chance to speak.*
- *Summarize decisions and check who is going to do what.*

Open an informal meeting.
Right, shall we get started?

Close an informal meeting.
Well, I think that covers everything ...

Define these things: an agenda / minutes / a chairperson.
- *the topics for a meeting*
- *a summary of the points discussed and decisions made at a meeting*
- *the person in charge of a meeting*

Think of a polite way of interrupting someone who is speaking.
- *Excuse me, could I just come in here?*
- *Sorry, can I just interrupt for a moment?*

You are interrupted during a meeting. Think of two phrases you could use to come back to the point you were making.
- *As I was saying ...*
- *Picking up where I left off, ...*

Think of two ways of disagreeing politely with someone at a meeting.
- *I'm not sure about that.*
- *Yes, but what about ...?*
- *Right. On the other hand, ...*

Describe a meeting you have recently attended.
(personalized response)

Card set 4: *Hazards*

A younger member of your team is dressed inappropriately for an international sales meeting, but he is your boss's nephew. Suggest a change or two.
- *Er, these meetings are usually pretty formal. I'd ...*
- *I think you'll find that most people will be wearing ...*

Your car has been broken into shortly before an important meeting in France. All your luggage has been stolen, including your briefcase and diary.
I'd ask if someone at the French company could give the local police a description of the missing things for me, then I'd phone my company to fax me my appointments ...

Your next project involves cooperating with colleagues from your subsidiary in Japan. You know very little about the country and its culture.
I'd ...

You have been asked to speak at a conference in West Africa. Your doctor has advised you not to travel there for health reasons.
I'd ...

Owing to an emergency, you have not yet completed your monthly report. It is due tomorrow morning, but the MD wants it this afternoon.
I'd ...

A fire in your regular supplier's warehouse has destroyed electronic components you have been waiting for. Without these you cannot meet a delivery deadline.
I'd ...

Your boss's retirement party is due to start in half an hour. You can't find the gold watch the department has bought him.
I'd ...

You are at a hotel bar making jokes about Americans with an Italian colleague. The man next to you turns around. He is your Chicago line manager.
I'd ...

You have personal reasons for disliking a director. Now you have been offered a promotion which would mean working closely with him or her.
I'd ...

"I've finished all my managing for today, Miss Withers, so I'm going home early."

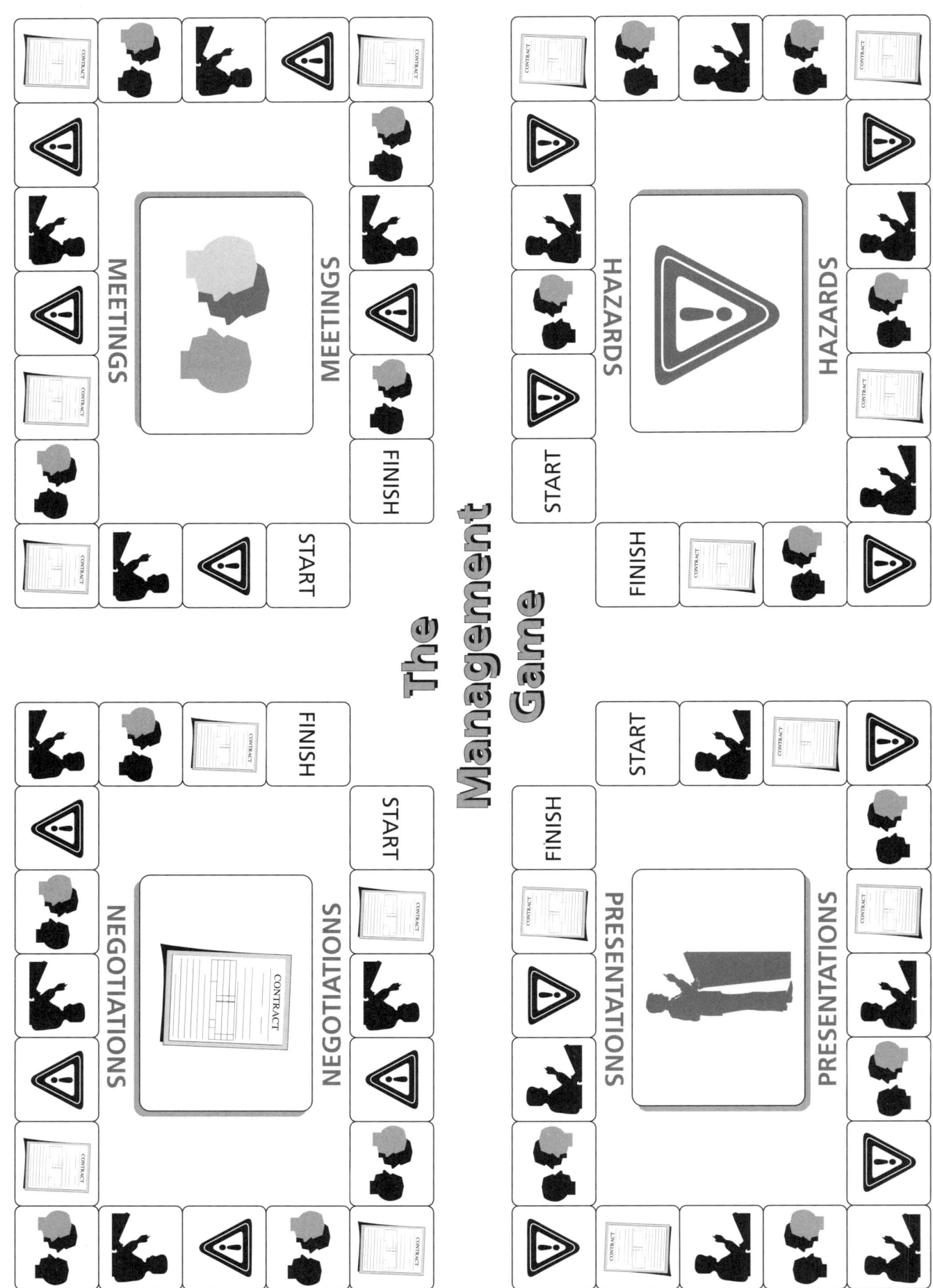

Introduce the guest speaker at an international conference.

Talk about equipment for presentations.

Give your opinion on what makes a good presentation.

Describe two mistakes that presenters sometimes make.

When might you use these expressions in a presentation? Now let's look at ...; As can you see ...

You are attending a presentation. Ask for more information about a particular point.

Someone tries to catch you out with a difficult question during a presentation.

At the end of a presentation, someone asks a question you can't answer.

Thank a presenter.

Comment on this statement: "It's better to be the buyer than the seller in a negotiation."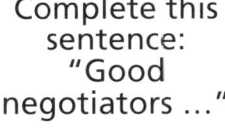

Complete this sentence: "Good negotiators ..."

Think of at least four words in the "negotiate" word family.

Think of at least three verbs that can be used with the word "contract" (e.g. to negotiate a contract).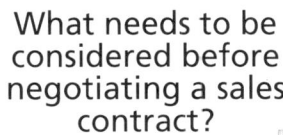

What needs to be considered before negotiating a sales contract?

The price you have been quoted for some new office equipment is far too high. Negotiate a reduction.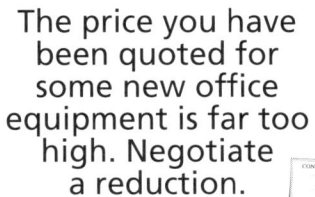

Your company hires out executive jets. Explain your terms to a customer using two of these expressions: as a rule / on condition that / even if / unless

Your boss has asked you to sort out a problem in a difficult country. This will take at least nine months. What terms would you negotiate?

Your assistant may resign unless he or she is given a substantial rise. This would be difficult at present. Negotiate a solution.

Think of at least three verbs that can be used with the word "meeting" (e.g. to organize a meeting).

One of your colleagues has to chair an important meeting for the first time. Give him or her three tips.

Open an informal meeting.

Close an informal meeting.

Define these things: an agenda / minutes / a chairperson.

Think of a polite way of interrupting someone who is speaking.

You are interrupted during a meeting. Think of two phrases you could use to come back to the point you were making.

Think of two ways of disagreeing politely with someone at a meeting.

Describe a meeting you have recently attended.

A younger member of your team is dressed inappropriately for an international sales meeting, but he is your boss's nephew. Suggest a change or two.

Your car has been broken into shortly before an important meeting in France. All your luggage has been stolen, including your briefcase and diary.

Your next project involves cooperating with colleagues from your subsidiary in Japan. You know very little about the country and its culture.

You have been asked to speak at a conference in West Africa. Your doctor has advised you not to travel there for health reasons.

Owing to an emergency, you have not yet completed your monthly report. It is due tomorrow morning, but the MD wants it this afternoon.

A fire in your regular supplier's warehouse has destroyed electronic components you have been waiting for. Without these you cannot meet a delivery deadline. Negotiate a reduction.

Your boss's retirement party is due to start in half an hour. You can't find the gold watch the department has bought him.

You are at a hotel bar making jokes about Americans with an Italian colleague. The man next to you turns around. He is your Chicago line manager.

You have personal reasons for disliking a director. Now you have been offered a promotion which would mean working closely with him or her.

The Office Communication Game

a Business English game

In this game learners practise typical office communication skills.

Language

Level
from lower intermediate

Telephoning
- checking and clarifying information
- giving and taking messages and information
- making appointments
- spelling
- taking and making calls
- telephone numbers

Figures
- cardinal numbers
- date
- price
- size and dimensions

Visitors
- business meals
- explaining and apologizing
- giving directions
- introductions
- talking about jobs and responsibilities
- welcoming visitors and making small talk

Paperwork
- standard openings and closes
- standard vocabulary and phrases

Preparation

Before the lesson
This game uses 4 different packs of cards: *Telephoning*, *Figures*, *Visitors* and *Paperwork*. Each pack contains 9 cards. Look at the cards on pages 97–98 and decide whether you want to use them or make your own using the blank cards on page 112.

You will need
- one A3-size photocopy of the board on page 96 per group of 4 learners;
- one cut-up set of the cards on pages 97–98 (or your own cards) per group;
- one dice per group;
- one marker per player.

The Game

Introduction
Divide learners into groups of 4 (one player for each corner of the board). Give each group a board, dice, markers and a full set of 36 cards.

Ask learners to gather round one board. Place the 4 packs of cards face down on the board. Demonstrate the game by making one or two moves and eliciting appropriate responses (see **Key** for suggestions).

The aim of the game
The winner is the first player to reach FINISH. You may wish to set a time limit rather than wait for a player to reach the middle of the board. The winner is then the player who has made the most moves.

How to play
Each player chooses a corner of the board and places his or her marker on START. The first player to throw a 6 begins. Players take it in turns to throw the dice and move around their corner of the board.

Players landing on a square take the top card from the appropriate pack, read it out and respond accordingly, interacting with a partner if necessary. If the rest of the group approve of the response, the game proceeds; if not, the player returns to his or her previous position.

Key
(some possible responses)

Card set 1: *Telephoning*

You are on the phone. You have to connect someone. What do you say?
- *Just a moment, please.*
- *Hold the line, please.*

You are on the phone. You want to speak to someone but she isn't in the office. Leave a message.
- *Could you tell Ms ... I called, please?*
- *My name's ... I'll call back later.*

You are on the phone. Make an appointment to meet someone.
- *Is Ms ... free on Monday?;*
- *How about Tuesday morning?*

You are on the phone. Explain politely that someone is not there.
I'm afraid Mr ... isn't in today. Can I take a message?

You are on the phone. Check the caller's name.
- *Could you repeat your name, please?*
- *Could you spell that, please?*

Give someone your office telephone number.
My office number is 01359 48006, extension 165.

You answer the phone. The caller asks to speak to you. What do you say? *Speaking.*

You can't hear a caller clearly. What do you say?
I'm afraid it's a bad line. Could you speak up a bit?

You want to check that you've written some information down correctly. What do you say?
Can I just read that back?

Card set 2: *Figures*

Talk about the price and delivery time of a product.
The ... costs £999. We can deliver at the end of the month.

Order a product. Include the quantity and ask about a discount.
I'd like to place an order for 555 ... The catalogue number is ... What sort of discount can you offer?

Say these numbers: 2,742; 2.472; 27%
Two thousand, seven hundred (and) forty-two; two point four seven two; twenty-seven per cent

Give some information about a piece of equipment, including size and weight.
The ... model is ... long and ... high. It weighs ...

Tell someone what your office hours are.
We're open from Monday to Friday from eight thirty to twelve and Tuesday and Thursday afternoon from three to six.

How would the British and Americans read this date: 1.4?
- *April 1st (GB)*
- *January 4th (US)*

Give a visitor some statistics about a company.
- *We employ ... people here.*
- *Last year our sales to ... were more than ...*
- *About ...% of our total production is exported to ...*

Say these prices: $859.23; ¥3,000,000,000
Eight hundred (and) fifty-nine dollars (and) twenty-three cents; three billion yen

Give some figures for two of these things: inflation, unemployment, the interest rate, the dollar.
The inflation rate is about ...% at the moment.
The dollar's at about ¥... in New York this morning.

Card set 3: *Visitors*

Introduce a visitor to a colleague.
This is Ms ... She's from ... She works for ...

Ask a visitor about their journey to your company.
- *Did you have a good flight?*
- *Did you have any trouble finding us?*

Make a visitor feel at home in your office.
- *Please sit down. / Take a seat, please.*
- *Can I offer you a cup of coffee? / Would you like something to drink?*

You are at reception. Give a visitor directions to someone's office.
Mr ...'s office is on the third floor. It's the second door on the right.

Say what you like (or don't like) about your job.
It's very interesting. I like my colleagues and I like the contact with customers.

Invite a visitor to have lunch in your canteen and describe a local dish.
- *Would you like to have lunch in the canteen?*
- *We've got ... on the menu today. It's a local speciality/a sort of ...*

Your boss has asked you to introduce a visitor to the people in your office. You can't remember his/her name!
- *This is Mr/Ms ... I'm so sorry – how do you pronounce your name?*
- *This is Mr/Ms ... I'm afraid I've forgotten your name.*

You are having lunch in the canteen with a visitor. He/She lights a cigarette in the no-smoking area.
Excuse me, but I'm afraid this is a no-smoking area. Let's move to ...

You pour out coffee for a visitor and spill some on his/her trousers.
Oh, dear! I'm so sorry! I'll just get a cloth ...

Card set 4: *Paperwork*

How do you begin a letter to a company when you don't know any names?
(GB) Dear Sirs; (US) Gentlemen:

A letter begins: "Thank you for the prompt delivery of our order No. 6502. However, item No. 12 is missing." Which department do you give this to?
Dispatch or sales department.

What type of letter does this sentence come from? "I enclose a CV with details of my experience in marketing."
An application for a job.

Think of two ways you could complete this phrase from a letter: "I look forward to …"
… seeing you/meeting you/hearing from you/your reply.

How would you write, "I'm sorry" in a business letter? *We regret …*

Name three words or expressions that you can find in most orders.
quantity; unit price; total amount

What closing phrase would you use in a business letter?
- *If you know the addressee's name: Yours sincerely (GB); Sincerely (yours) (US)*
- *If you don't the addressee's name: Yours faithfully (GB); Yours truly, / Truly yours, (US)*

What does "p.p." mean in a business letter?
per pro = someone else has signed for the person who wrote the letter.

How could you say this phrase from a business letter in one word?
"We would be grateful if you could … "
Please …

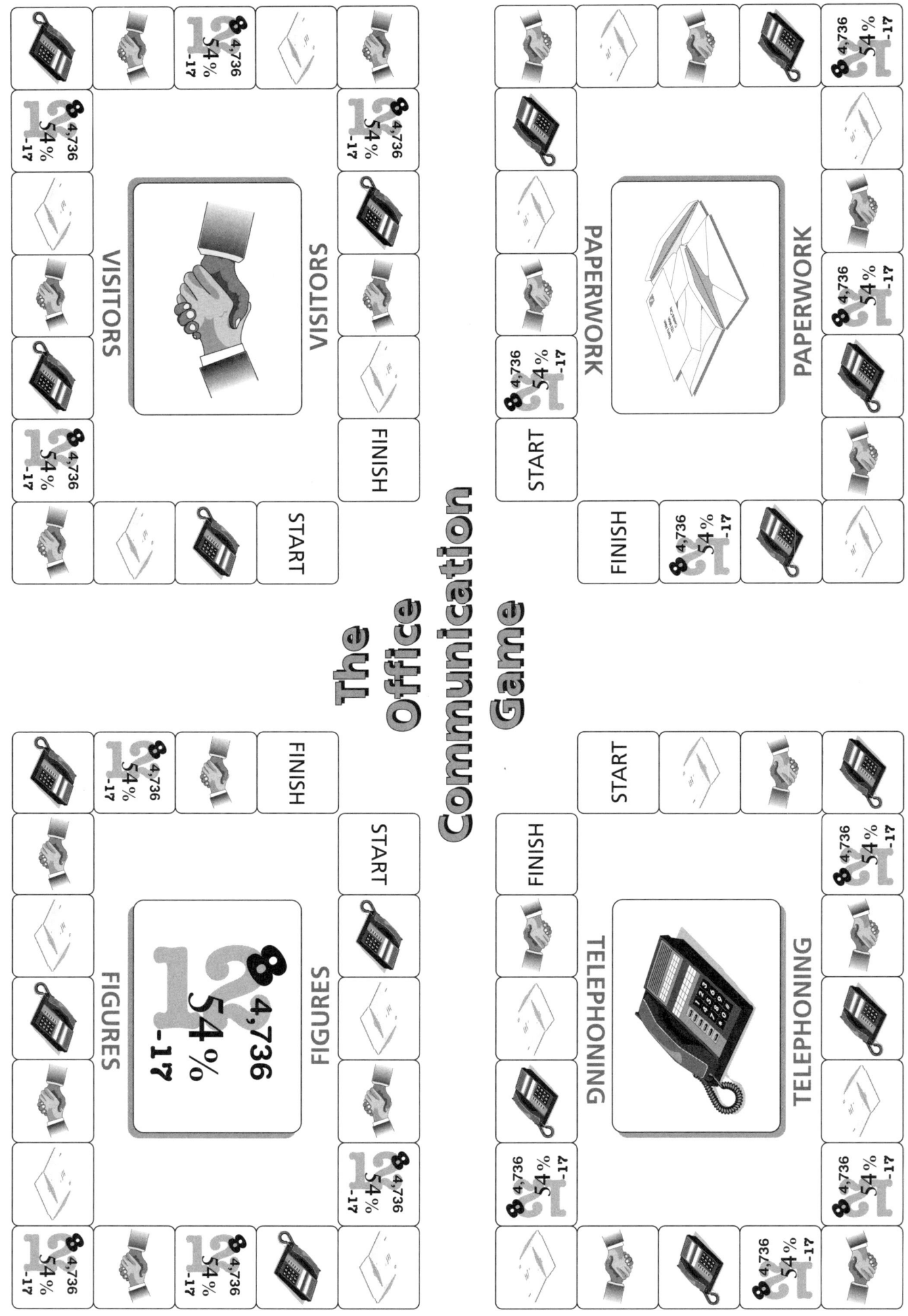

The Office Communication Game

VISITORS

FINISH

START

PAPERWORK

START

FINISH

FIGURES

FINISH

START

TELEPHONING

START

FINISH

You are on the phone. You have to connect someone. What do you say?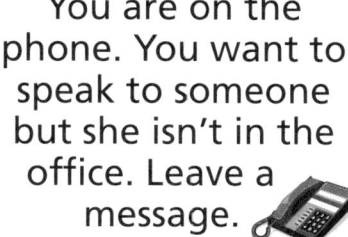

You are on the phone. You want to speak to someone but she isn't in the office. Leave a message.

You are on the phone. Make an appointment to meet someone.

You are on the phone. Explain politely that someone is not there.

You are on the phone. Check the caller's name.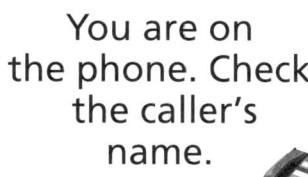

Give someone your office telephone number.

You answer the phone. The caller asks to speak to you. What do you say?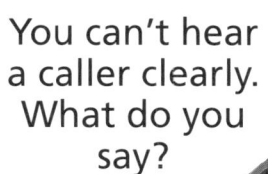

You can't hear a caller clearly. What do you say?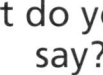

You want to check that you've written some information down correctly. What do you say?

Talk about the price and delivery time of a product. ♻ 4,736 54% -17

Order a product. Include the quantity and ask about a discount. ♻ 4,736 54% -17

Say these numbers: 2,742; 2.472; 27% ♻ 4,736 54% -17

Give some information about a piece of equipment, including size and weight. ♻ 4,736 54% -17

Tell someone what your office hours are. ♻ 4,736 54% -17

How would the British and Americans read this date: 1.4? ♻ 4,736 54% -17

Give a visitor some statistics about a company. ♻ 4,736 54% -17

Say these prices: $859.23; ¥3,000,000,000 ♻ 4,736 54% -17

Give some figures for two of these things: inflation, unemployment, the interest rate, the dollar. ♻ 4,736 54% -17

The Office Communication Game · Cards

Introduce a visitor to a colleague. 	Ask a visitor about their journey to your company. 	Make a visitor feel at home in your office. 
You are at reception. Give a visitor directions to someone's office. 	Say what you like (or don't like) about your job. 	Invite a visitor to have lunch in your canteen and describe a local dish. 
Your boss has asked you to introduce a visitor to people in your office. You can't remember his/her name!	You are having lunch in the canteen with a visitor. He/She lights a cigarette in the non-smoking area. 	You pour out coffee for a visitor and spill some on his/her trousers. 
How do you begin a letter to a company when you don't know any names?	A letter begins: "Thank you for the prompt delivery of our order No. 6502. However, item No. 12 is missing." Which department do you give this to?	What type of letter does this sentence come from? "I enclose a CV with details of my experience in marketing."
Think of two ways you could complete this phrase from a letter: "I look forward to …"	How would you write, "I'm sorry" in a business letter?	Name three words or expressions that you can find in most orders.
What closing phrase would you use in a business letter?	What does "p.p." mean in a business letter?	How could you say this phrase from a business letter in one word? "We would be grateful if you could …"

The Office Communication Game · Cards

The Socializing Game

a Business English game

In this game learners practise the language of social interaction for their jobs.

Language

Level
from lower intermediate

Functions
- apologizing
- dealing with visitors' problems: lost items, etc.
- describing how things work
- explaining company rules and regulations
- giving directions: indoors and outdoors
- introductions and greetings
- making, accepting and refusing invitations
- problem situations: forgetting to do things; reminding others to do things, etc.
- talking about health
- talking about hobbies and interests
- talking about oneself
- talking about the local area, people, customs, etc.
- talking about the weather

Preparation

You will need
- one A3-size photocopy of the board on page 102 per group of 4–6 learners;
- one dice per group;
- one marker per player.

The Game

Introduction
Divide learners into groups of 4–6 players. Give each group a board, dice and markers.

Ask learners to gather round one board. Demonstrate the game by making one or two moves and eliciting appropriate responses (see **Key** for suggestions).

The aim of the game
The winner is the first player to reach FINISH. You may wish to set a time limit rather than wait for a player to reach the final square. The winner is then the player who has made the most moves.

How to play
Players place their markers on START. The first player to throw a 6 begins. Players take it in turns to throw the dice and move around the board.

Players landing on a square respond accordingly, interacting with a partner if necessary. If the rest of the group approve of the response, the game proceeds; if not, the player returns to his or her previous position.

Key
(some possible reponses)

1. Greet a colleague in the morning.
   Morning, John. How are you?

2. Introduce a visitor from America.
   - *This is ... She's from ...*
   - *... 's here for the ... meeting and ...*

3. Introduce yourself briefly to an international group.
   - *My name's ... I come from ...*
   - *I'm a ... and I've been working for/in the ... department for ... years.*

4. Welcome a group of visitors to your department or company.
   - *Well, my name's ... and I'd like to welcome you to ...*
   - *Can I offer you something to drink? We've got tea, coffee, soft drinks ...*

5. Talk about your daily routine.
   - *I usually spend a lot of time on the phone.*
   - *I always have lunch in the canteen.*

6. Describe where you come from or where you live.
   - *I come from ... It's a small town near ... with a population of ...*
   - *I live in ... It's about the same size as ...*

7. Collect a visitor from reception and accompany him/her to the conference room.
   - *Mr/Ms ...? Good morning. I'm ...*
   - *Would you like to come with me?*
   - *The conference room is on the third floor. We'll take the lift.*
   - *How was your journey?*

8. Your boss will be meeting a client at the airport. Describe her to the client.
   She's about 35, tall with fair hair and glasses ...

9. Accept an invitation to lunch with a business partner.
   Thank you very much. That's very kind of you. I'd love to.

10. Apologize for spilling beer on a visitor's trousers.
    Oh, dear! I'm so sorry! I'll just a get a cloth ...

11. Describe your job.
    - *I'm a … I work in the … department of a large … company.*
    - *I'm responsible for …*

12. Invite a visitor for lunch.
    - *Would you like to join me for lunch?*
    - *How about lunch in the canteen?*

13. Explain how to use the local transport system.
    - *The system's easy. You can use the same ticket for buses and trains.*
    - *There are different tickets: for the whole day, for single journeys or for several.*
    - *You can get tickets on the bus or from a machine, but not on the train.*

14. Refuse an invitation to lunch.
    - *I'd love to come, but I've got another meeting in about an hour.*
    - *I'm sorry, but I'm …*

15. A visitor is unhappy with her hotel.
    - *I'm sorry to hear that.*
    - *Our visitors usually stay there and we've never had a complaint before.*
    - *Would you like me to find you another hotel?*

16. Describe a local dish to a foreign visitor.
    - *It's made of …*
    - *It's a sort of …*
    - *It's baked/fried/smoked/boiled/roast …*

17. Describe a company regulation to a visitor.
    - *We're not allowed to work more than 42 hours a week.*
    - *We don't get paid for overtime, we have to take the time off.*

18. A Japanese visitor wants to buy some souvenirs for his family.
    - *How old are your children?*
    - *Are they interested in …?*
    - *What about a T-shirt with a picture of … on it?*

19. A client has a bad headache.
    - *Oh dear! Can I get you an aspirin?*
    - *What about something stronger?*
    - *It's probably the weather.*

20. Explain how a piece of office equipment works.
    - *You put your letter in here, upside down.*
    - *Type in the number and then press the green button.*

21. Suggest how visitors could spend an evening in your town.
    - *If you like sport, you could play some tennis or squash.*
    - *You can hire tennis things from/at …*
    - *Why not go out for a meal and then walk around the old town …*

22. Cancel a lunch invitation.
    - *I'm very sorry, but I'm afraid I have to cancel our lunch tomorrow.*
    - *I've got so much to do at the moment. Maybe we could meet on …*

23. Your host has just asked for the bill, but you want to pay for this meal.
    - *That's very kind of you but I'd like to pay for this.*
    - *No, no. This one is on me.*

24. Talk about a hobby.
    - *I'm very interested in …*
    - *I belong to a … club and we meet/play every week/once a month.*

25. Explain a local custom to a visitor.
    - *On the first of May every year people dance and sing in the streets.*
    - *They dance around the figure of a black horse with a man inside. They sing about the end of winter and the beginning of summer.*

26. Give directions to an office in another building.
    - *Go out through the main door, turn left and it's the red building opposite.*
    - *Mr …'s office is on the second floor, the third door on the right.*

27. You're at a meeting and don't feel well. Explain your problem.
    - *I'm afraid I don't feel very well. I think I'm getting flu.*
    - *Could you ask … to get me some medicine from the chemist's?*

28. A client's handbag has been stolen.
    - *When did you last see it?*
    - *Can you describe it?*
    - *We'll have to go to the police station.*

29. Talk about a local personality.
    He's the mayor of … and he's very interested in local problems.

30. Thank someone for helping you.
    - *Thank you very much.*
    - *It was very kind of you.*

31. Apologize for a colleague's absence.
    - *I'm afraid Ms … can't come to the meeting.*
    - *She's ill, I'm afraid. She sends her apologies.*

32. Complain about your hotel room.

My room's very noisy. It faces the main road. Could I have a quieter room, please?

33. Explain how to get to a local place of interest.
    * *You can walk there, it's not far from here.*
    * *You walk straight down ... and turn right at the ...*
    * *You can't miss it. It's a yellow building with lots of windows.*

34. Tell a new colleague about your working hours.
    * *We have flexitime here. That means we can begin any time between 7.00 and 8.30 and leave between 4.00 and 7.00.*

35. You know your Australian colleague is very busy, but you need his help.
    * *I'm very sorry to bother you, but ...*
    * *I know you've got a lot to do at the moment, but ...*

36. You're on a business trip and you can't find your briefcase.
    * *I think I've lost my briefcase. It's a black ...*
    * *My diary and all the materials for my presentation are in it!*

* *Could you possibly phone ... for me? Maybe I left it there.*

37. You are saying goodbye to a client. Send greetings to someone you both know.
    Give my regards to ...

38. At a conference you meet someone you think you've met before. Find out where.
    * *Haven't we met before?*
    * *You're ..., aren't you?*
    * *We met at the conference ..., didn't we?*

39. Comment on the weather.
    Very cold this morning. Much colder than it was in ...

40. A visitor breaks a cup in your office.
    * *It doesn't matter.*

"This is Hodgkinson – he's in charge of the shredder."

THE SOCIALIZING GAME

START

- Greet a colleague in the morning.
- Introduce a visitor from America.
- Introduce yourself briefly to an international group.
- Welcome a group of visitors to your department or company.
- Talk about your daily routine.
- Describe where you come from or where you live.
- Collect a visitor from reception and accompany him/her to the conference room.
- Your boss will be meeting a client at the airport. Describe her to the client.
- Accept an invitation to lunch with a business partner.
- Apologize for spilling beer on a visitor's trousers.

- A client's handbag has been stolen.
- You're at a meeting and don't feel well. Explain your problem.
- Give directions to an office in another building.
- Explain a local custom to a visitor.
- Talk about a hobby.

- Talk about a local personality.
- Thank someone for helping you.
- Apologize for a collleague's absence.
- Complain about your hotel room.
- Explain how to get to a local place of interest.
- Tell a new colleague about your working hours.
- You know your Australian colleague is very busy, but you need his help.
- Describe your job.

- Your host has just asked for the bill, but you want to pay for this meal.
- Cancel a lunch invitation.
- Suggest how visitors could spend an evening in your town.
- Explain how a piece of office equipment works.
- A client has a bad headache.
- A Japanese visitor wants to buy some souvenirs for his family.
- Describe a company regulation to a visitor.
- Describe a local dish to a foreign visitor.
- A visitor is unhappy with her hotel.
- Refuse an invitation for lunch.
- Explain how to use the local transport system.
- You are saying goodbye to a client. Send greetings to someone you both know.
- You're on a business trip and you can't find your briefcase.
- Invite a visitor for lunch.

- A visitor breaks a cup in your office.
- Comment on the weather.
- At a conference you meet someone you think you've met before. Find out where.

FINISH

GAME

The Telephoning Game

a Business English game

In this game learners practise standard telephone phrases.

Language

Level
from lower intermediate

Telephone phrases
- answering machines
- bad lines, wrong numbers and other problems
- checking and clarifying information
- getting through to the right person
- giving and leaving messages
- making and taking calls
- putting through

Preparation

Before the lesson
Look at the tasks for this game on the board (page 105) and the cards (page 106). If you want to add tasks personalized to your learners' work, use the spare cards.

You will need
- one A3-size photocopy of the board on page 105 per group of 4–6 learners;
- one cut-up set of the cards on page 106 per group;
- one dice per group;
- one marker per player.

The Game

Introduction
Divide learners into groups of 4–6 players. Give each group a board, dice and markers and a set of cards.

Ask learners to gather round one board. Place the cards face down on the board. Demonstrate the game by making one or two moves and eliciting appropriate responses (see **Key** for suggestions).

The aim of the game
The winner is the first player to reach FINISH. You may wish to set a time limit rather than wait for a player to reach the final square. The winner is then the player who has made the most moves.

How to play
Players place their markers on START. The first player to throw a 6 begins. Players take it in turns to throw the dice and move around the board.

A player landing on a square with a task reads it out and responds accordingly. If the rest of the group approve of the response, the game proceeds; if not, the player returns to his or her previous position.

Players landing on a square with a telephone symbol take the top card from the pack, read it out and respond accordingly.

Key
(some possible responses)

Tasks on the board

1. Ask for someone on the telephone by name.
   - *Can I speak to ..., please?*
   - *I'd like to speak to ...*

2. A caller asks to speak to you.
   Speaking.

4. Give someone a telephone number.
   (e.g.) *Oh one seven one – three nine five – two nine double-five*

5. Ask a caller to spell her/his name.
   Could you spell that, please?

6. A caller wants to speak to someone who isn't in today. Offer to give them some information.
   - *Can I take a message?*
   - *Would you like to leave a message?*

8. Say why you are calling.
   I'm calling about ...

9. Identify yourself on the telephone.
   - *This is ... from ...*
   - *Hello, it's ... from ... here.*

11. Check that you've written down a message correctly.
    - *Let me read that back.*
    - *Can I just check I've got that right?*

12. Ask a caller to dial you again.
    Could you try calling again?

14. Check that you've got the right number.
    Is that ...?

15. The person a caller wants to speak to is calling someone else.
    I'm afraid the line's busy.

16. Ask a caller to wait.
    - *One moment, please.*
    - *Hold on, please.*
    - *Hold the line, please.*

18. Ask if a caller wants to wait.
    - *Would you like to hold?*
    - *Shall I put you on hold?*

19. You're going on a business trip. Say where someone can call you.
    She/He can reach me on …

20. The person you want to speak to is at lunch. Say you'll try again during the afternoon.
    I'll call back later.

22. Answer the phone at work.
    (Williams & Hunt), good morning/afternoon.

23. Spell a colleague's name.
    (I'll spell that), that's …

24. Thank someone for telephoning you.
    Thank you for calling.

25. Leave a message on an answering machine.
    This is … from … Could you call me back on …, please?

27. Someone wants to speak to your boss. You need to know why.
    - *Can I tell him/her why you're calling?*
    - *May I ask the purpose of your call?*

28. Ask a caller to identify himself/herself.
    - *Who's calling, please?*
    - *Could I have your name, please?*

30. You receive a call for one of your colleagues. Tell the caller and connect them.
    The best person to speak would be Mr/Ms …
    I'll put you through.

31. The person you want to speak to is out. You want them to call you when they get back.
    Could you ask him/her to call me back?

32. A caller asks to speak to one of your colleagues. No one picks up the phone.
    I'm afraid there's no answer. (Can I help you, perhaps?)

34. Ask a caller for their telephone number.
    - *Could I have your number, please?*
    - *What number is it, please?*
    - *Where can we reach you?*

35. Ask the person who answers the phone to transfer you to someone else.
    Could you put me through to …, please?

36. Apologize for causing someone inconvenience.
    Sorry to bother you.

37. A caller thanks you for your help. Reply.
    - *You're welcome.*
    - *My pleasure.*
    - *That's OK.*

39. Reassure a caller that you will do something urgently.
    Leave it with me. I'll deal with it right away.

40. Work out a message for an answering machine for your department.
    This is (Williams & Hunt). I'm afraid no one is available to take your call at the moment. Please leave your name and number and we'll call you back as soon as our office reopens. Thank you for calling.

Tasks on the cards

Ask a caller to say something again.
Could you repeat that, please?

You dial a number but someone at a different number answers.
Oh, I'm sorry! I've dialled the wrong number.

A caller is speaking too fast.
Could you speak a bit more slowly, please?

The line goes dead in the middle of a call. Call back and explain.
We were cut off.

Tell a caller that you can't hear them at all.
I'm afraid it's a terrible line.

A caller is speaking too quietly.
Could you speak up a bit, please?

A caller asks something that you are not sure about.
- *I'll check that and call you back.*
- *Can I get back to you on that?*

You didn't hear a number properly.
- *Sorry, I didn't catch that.*
- *Was that …?*

The phone rings. You pick it up but you can't hear anything.
Hello?

Someone calls you but does not say what they want. Find out.
- *What can I do for you?*
- *How can I help you?*

THE TELEPHONING GAME

START

Ask for someone on the telephone by name.

A caller asks to speak to you.

Give someone a telephone number.

Ask a caller to spell her/his name.

A caller wants to speak to someone who isn't in today. Offer to give them some information.

Say why you are calling.

Identify yourself on the telephone.

Ask a caller to identify himself/herself.

Someone wants to speak to your boss. You need to know why.

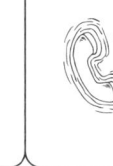

You receive a call for one of your colleagues. Tell the caller and connect them.

The person you want to speak to is out. You want them to call you when they get back.

A caller asks to speak to one of your colleagues. No one picks up the phone.

Ask a caller for their telephone number.

Ask the person who answers the phone to transfer you to someone else.

Apologize for causing someone inconvenience.

A caller thanks you for help. Reply.

Check that you've written down a message correctly.

Ask a caller to dial you again.

Leave a message on an answering machine.

Thank someone for telephoning you.

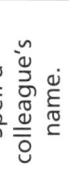

Spell a colleague's name.

Answer the phone at work.

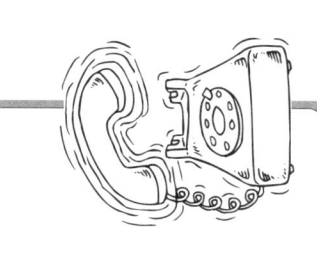

FINISH

Work out a message for an answering machine for your department.

Reassure a caller that you will do something urgently.

GAME

The person you want to speak to is at lunch. Say you'll try again during the afternoon.

You're going on a business trip. Say where someone can call you.

Ask if a caller wants to wait.

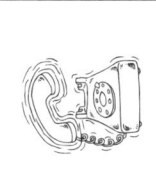

Ask a caller to wait.

Check that you've got the right number.

The person a caller wants to speak to is calling someone else.

Ask a caller to say something again.	You dial a number but someone at a different number answers.	A caller is speaking too fast.
The line goes dead in the middle of a call. Call back and explain.	Tell a caller that you can't hear them at all.	A caller is speaking too quietly.
A caller asks something that you are not sure about.	You didn't hear a number properly.	The phone rings. You pick it up but you can't hear anything.
Someone calls you but does not say what they want. Find out.		

The Working Day Game

a Business English game

In this game learners practise English for everyday situations at work.

Language

Level
from lower intermediate

Topics
- Typical job-related language, e.g.
- dealing with visitors
- describing a company
- describing jobs
- talking about work activities

Preparation

Before the lesson
Decide whether you want to use the cards on page 110–111 or make your own using the blank cards on page 112.

You will need
- one A3-size photocopy of the board on page 109 per group of 4–6 learners;
- one cut-up set of the cards on pages 110–111 (or your own cards) per group;
- one dice per group;
- one marker per player.

The Game

Introduction
Divide learners into groups of 4–6 players. Give each group a board, dice and a set of cards.

Ask learners to gather round one board. Place the cards face down on the board. Demonstrate the game by making one or two moves and eliciting appropriate responses (see **Key** for suggestions).

The aim of the game
The winner is the player who circles the board first. You may wish to set a time limit rather than wait for a player to return to his or her starting position; the winner is then the player who has made the most moves.

How to play
Players place their markers on the time they normally start work (or their favourite time of day). The first player to throw a 6 begins. Players take it in turns to throw the dice and move clockwise around the board.

Players landing on a square take the top card from the pack, read it out and respond accordingly, interacting with a partner if necessary. If the rest of the group approve of the response, the game proceeds; if not, the player returns to his or her previous position.

Key

(some possible responses)

When do you start and finish work?
I start at 8.30 and work until 4 p.m. every day.

How do you get to work?
By train. I leave home at … and walk to the station. I catch the … train and …

Talk about flexitime in your company.
- *You can start work between … and ….*
- *Everybody has to be at work between … and …*
- *We don't have flexitime. Everybody has to …*

What do you do when you arrive at work?
Sort the post, make coffee, talk to colleagues ….

Are there any rules about what you wear to work?
- *No. We can wear anything!*
- *Yes, we mustn't wear jeans and T-shirts!*

What are your overtime rules?
- *We aren't paid for overtime.*
- *We can do 10 hours a month …*

Tell an English colleague about your canteen.
- *Lunch is from 11.30 to 2.*
- *Meals cost about …*
- *Each week you have to say if you want lunch the following week.*

Describe a typical meal in your canteen.
A typical meal is roast pork, salad and sort of bread dumplings.

Describe a colleague so that a visitor can recognize him/her.
She's about 35, quite tall and slim. She's got long, reddish, curly hair and she wears glasses.

Describe your office
- *It's not very large. There's a desk, two cupboards and a photocopier.*
- *I share it with three other people. My desk is next to the window and there's a …*

Describe your company.
- *Our headquarters are in …*
- *We have … employees.*
- *We manufacture …*

Explain what you do.
- *I work in the ... department. I'm responsible for ...*
- *I'm the Sales Manager. I ...*

Direct a colleague to another office.
It's on the third floor, the second door on the right.

What do you keep in the drawers of your desk?
Scissors, punch, files, chocolate ...

Name four office machines.
Photocopier, printer, franking machine, typewriter

Give an example of a sentence from a letter you often have to write in English.
- *Thank you very much for ...*
- *If you have any further questions, please call me.*

Talk about a typical phone call you have to make in English.
- *I call people in the States about ...*
- *People call from Sydney and want information about ...*

Describe your first/last job.
- *My first job was in ...*
- *Before I came here I worked in a ...*

Explain what your group/department does.
We work in sales. We are responsible for the orders.

Tell an English-speaking caller where two colleagues are.
- *I'm afraid Ms ... isn't in this week. She's at a conference in ....*
- *Mr ...'s in a meeting. He'll be free at ...*

A caller needs the correct job titles of two colleagues.
- *Mr ... is our Sales Manager for Europe.*
- *Ms ... is Head of Human Resources.*

Find out when an English colleague wants to take his/her holiday so that you can plan yours.
When are you taking your holiday? I'd like to take the first two weeks in July ...

An English-speaking colleague says, "Have a good weekend!" What do you say?
You too!

Explain a company rule.
- *We have to go to lunch between ... and ...*
- *We're not allowed to ...*
- *We mustn't ...*

Talk about the departments in your company or a company you know.
We're a very small company. We've only got an administration and a sales department.

Talk about your company's "Wellness" programme. If you haven't got one, invent one!
- *We've got our own sports centre. You can play tennis and football or swim after work or at the weekends.*
- *There's a first-aid course and an anti-smoking therapy group ...*

Talk about a training course you have been on (or want to go on).
I did a telephoning course. We practised phone calls with difficult customers.

Talk about your boss's daily routine
He arrives about 10 a.m. First he deals with his post. Then he tells his secretary what needs to be done and starts making phone calls ...

Look after a foreign visitor who has to wait for your boss.
I'm afraid Mr... will be a little late. Would you like to take a seat? Can I get you something to drink?

Leave a message on an answering machine in England.
My name's ... from ... in ... Could Ms ... call me back, please? My number's ...

Give a telephone message about an appointment to an English-speaking colleague.
Ms ... called. She says she'll be in ... on Tuesday and would like to come and see you. Can you call her back? You've got her number.

Spell the name of a colleague.
(e.g. W I double L O U G H B Y)

Explain the hierachy in your company.
There's a president and a vice president. Each division has a manager who reports to the vice president.

Describe one of your company's products or services.
We produce software for insurance companies and banks.

What do you like best about your job?
I like working with people. Every day is different!

What is stressful about your job?
The long hours. I don't like working in the evening. And the customers...!

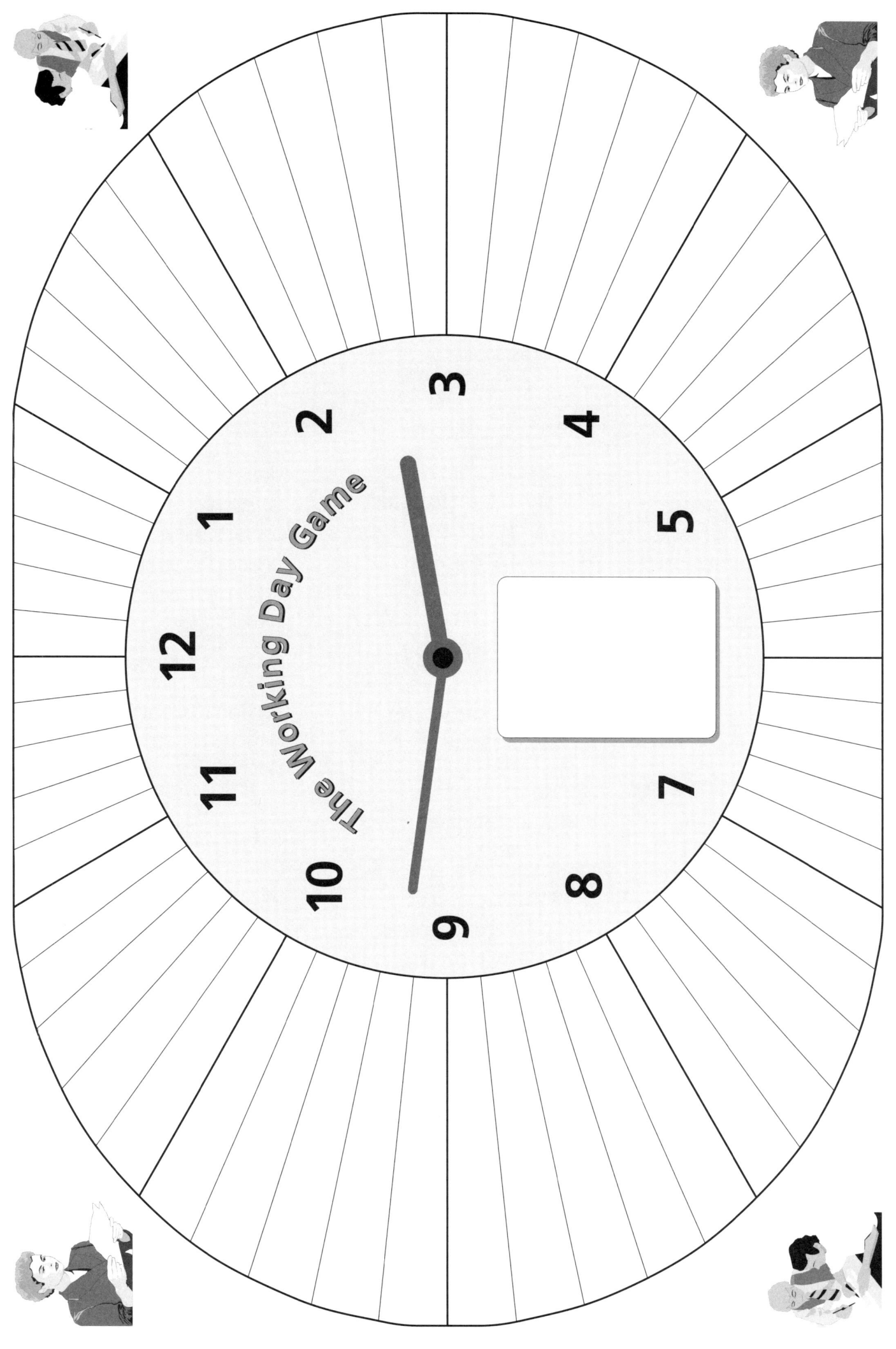

The Working Day Game · Board

When do you start and finish work?

How do you get to work?

Talk about flexi-time in your company.

What do you do when you arrive at work?

Are there any rules about what you wear to work?

What are your overtime rules?

Tell an English colleague about your canteen.

Describe a typical meal in your canteen.

Describe a colleague so that a visitor can recognize him/her.

Describe your office.

Describe your company.

Explain what you do.

Direct a colleague to another office.

What do you keep in the drawers of your desk?

Name four office machines.

Give an example of a sentence from a letter you often have to write in English.

Talk about a typical phone call you have to make in English.

Describe your first/last job.

Explain what your group/department does.

Tell an English-speaking caller where two colleagues are.

A caller needs the correct job titles of two colleagues.

Find out when an English colleague wants to take his/her holiday so that you can plan yours.

An English-speaking colleague says, "Have a good weekend!" What do you say?

Explain a company rule.

Talk about the departments in your company or a company you know.

Talk about your company's "Well-ness" programme. If you haven't got one, invent one!

Talk about a training course you have been on (or want to go on).

Talk about your boss's daily routine.

Look after a foreign visitor who has to wait for your boss.

Leave a message on an answering machine in England.

Give a telephone message about an appointment to an English colleague.

Spell the name of a colleague.

Explain the hierachy in your company.

Describe one of your company's products or services.

What do you like best about your job?

What is stressful about your job?

The Working Day Game · Cards   111